A Rainbow of

STITCHES

photography by
frédéric lucano

A Rainbow of
STITCHES

EMBROIDERY AND CROSS-STITCH BASICS
PLUS MORE THAN 1,000 MOTIFS AND 80 PROJECT IDEAS

agnès delage-calvet

anne sohier-fournel

muriel brunet

françoise ritz

watson-guptill publications / new york

Published in the United States by Watson-Guptill Publications,
an imprint of Crown Publishing Group
a division of Random House, Inc., New York

www.crownpublishing.com
www.watsonguptill.com

Watson-Guptill is a registered trademark and the WG and Horse
designs are trademarks of Random House, Inc.

Library of Congress Control Number: 2009927351
ISBN 978-0-8230-1478-1

Designer: Vera Fong
Stylist: Sonia Lucano

2 3 4 5 6 7 8/ 16 15 14 13 12 11 10 9

First Edition
Printed in Malaysia

contents

preface

If you haven't tried embroidery or cross-stitch before, a quick look through this book will give you overwhelming proof that you can stitch on virtually anything made from fabric. More than eighty beautifully photographed, inspiring ideas for stitched embellishment are shown, from wearables and personal accessories to a variety of decorative items for every room in your home.

Each section of the book, which is organized by color—green, pink, blue, red, and white (and taupe)—presents ideas for embroidering a range of accompanying motifs in single colors, showing how much impact you can get from working with just one color of floss on a plain background.

The prerequisites for stitching are simple and few. Start by choosing a motif from this extensive and exhaustive collection, which ranges from elegant alphabets to 1970s-inspired flowers and leaves, from sweet fairies to vintage-chic ladies in classic Dior dresses. The "Get Stitching" section gives you everything you need to know to get started: how to work with embroidery floss, fabric, needles, hoops, and how to transfer designs, along with an illustrated how-to of the simple stitches that are used to create all of the motifs shown in the book.

So dig through your closets and open your dresser drawers to find an item that needs a little extra "something," then take a trip to your local crafts or fabric store to get some basic supplies. A rainbow of stitches awaits!

get
stitching

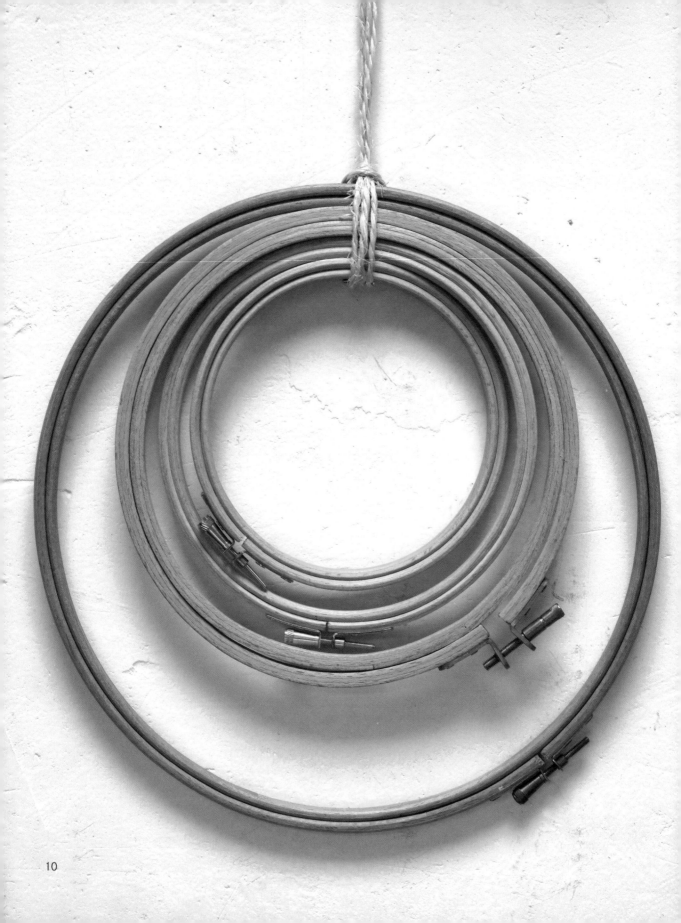

before you begin

Before you start, make sure your fabric is well prepared so it won't fray as you're stitching it. You can either hem the edges with a large basting stitch, or simply apply fusible web strips around the fabric's perimeter. Keep in mind that the piece of fabric should always be larger than the pattern to be stitched.

working with fabric

Fold your fabric in four to find its center point. Make large basting stitches along both the horizontal and vertical folds to serve as guidelines as you stitch. Align the center point of your motif with the point where the two lines of stitching intersect. Remove these guidelines once you've finished embroidering your motif.

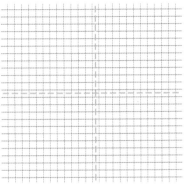

To help your stitches stay even, use an embroidery hoop. Gently stretch your fabric on the hoop, making sure to reposition it frequently—or to remove it at the end of each stitching session—to avoid damaging its weave.

working with embroidery floss

Two to three strands of six-strand cotton floss were used to stitch all of the projects shown in this book. Whenever you start a project, you'll find it helpful to make a sampler of stitches on the fabric you're planning to use to determine how many strands of floss you'll need. As a general rule, lower-count Aidas—a type of counted thread fabric that's traditionally used for cross-stitch projects—require more strands, while higher-count Aidas and linens need fewer. For example, most projects stitched on 14-count Aida require three strands of floss, while those stitched on a 28-count linen, which has a much tighter weave, would probably need just two strands, and even one might look fine.

transferring motifs

To transfer motifs to your fabric, use carbon transfer paper, which is specially made for embroidery and is available in several colors. Choose the one that works best with your fabric. For example, white transfer paper is best for dark fabrics, while blue or red work best on lighter ones.

Start by photocopying the motif, which you can enlarge or reduce to get it to just the right size. Trace the photocopied motif on a sheet of tracing paper, following its outline and making sure to include all its details. Prepare your fabric according to the instructions on the previous page, then iron it carefully before spreading it out on a flat surface, such as an ironing board or clean work table.

Place the transfer paper between the fabric and the tracing paper, making sure to put the colored side of the transfer paper face down. Keep the papers in place by pinning them to the fabric. With a hard pencil or a pen, carefully trace the motif, pressing down so that the entire image transfers properly. Once you've finished, separate the papers and fabric carefully to avoid smudging the fabric.

starting and ending off

This method of starting and ending off avoids having to tie knots on the back of your piece. To begin, take about a yard of floss, using as many strands as you need for your project. Fold it in two, then thread the needle. Bring the needle up through the fabric, leaving the loop created by the folded floss at the back. Bring the needle back down to start your first stitch, passing it through the loop, then pull gently to lock in the thread. Once you're done stitching, slip your thread under your last three or four stitches.

Before you begin, review the steps on the following pages. Even experienced stitchers are sure to find tips and hints to make their work easier.

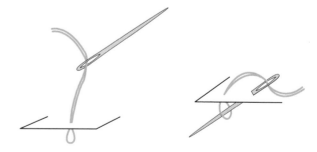

essential stitches

To embroider the motifs in this book, you'll need to learn just seven easy stitches. Most of the motifs use the stem stitch, except for some of the smaller details, which are noted in each motif.

CROSS STITCH METHOD 1

Cross stitches are typically worked on counted-thread fabric. This method is especially useful for lines of cross stitch.

Come up through the fabric at point A, then go back down at point B, up at C, down at D. Come back up at E and, working in the opposite direction, go down at B to form an X.

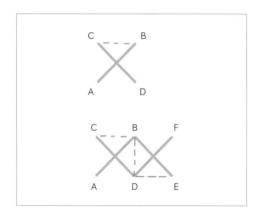

CROSS STITCH METHOD 2

This method can be used either for lines of cross stitch or to make individual stitches.

1. Come up at point A, go down at B, come back up at C, then down at D to form the first cross stitch.
2. Come back up at B, go down at E, come up at D, then go down at F to the second cross stitch.

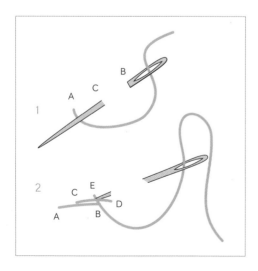

STEM STITCH

Stem stitches create a continuous yet slightly staggered line.

1. Bring the needle up at point A, then into B and up at C (midway between A and B). Note that the thread should loop under the needle.
2. To make the next stitch, go down at D and come back up at E, above the previous stitch and midway along its length.

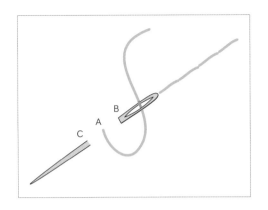

BACKSTITCH

Backstitching creates a continuous line of even stitches.

Bring the needle up at point A, down at B (the end of the previous stitch) and back up at C. To make the next stitch, bring the needle down at point A, then up at point C, and continue.

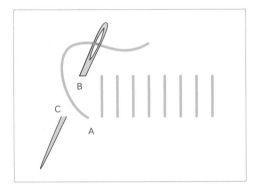

STRAIGHT STITCH

The straight stitch is the simplest of all stitches.

Bring the needle up at point A, then down at B, then come back at C. Be careful, stitches should not be too long. If needed, straight stitches can be aligned next to each other to fill areas with solid color.

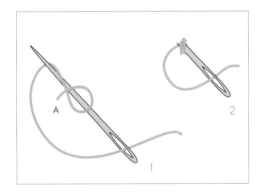

FRENCH KNOT

French knots can be used to make eyes, speckles, spots, and other small details.

1. Bring the needle up at point A. Hold the thread taut and wrap it around the needle twice.
2. Without letting go of the thread, go back down into A, slipping the needle through the wraps to form a knot.

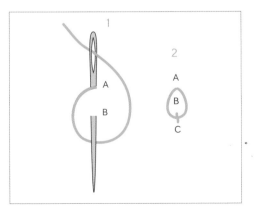

LAZY DAISY / CHAIN STITCH

A lazy daisy, or a detached chain stitch, can be worked singly; one after the other, in a continuous length; or arranged in a circle to create a flower.

1. Bring the needle up at point A. Form a loop, then go back in through A and down at B so that the needle passes over the loop.
2. Finish by going back down into the fabric at C (right below B), to make a tiny stitch to keep the loop in place.

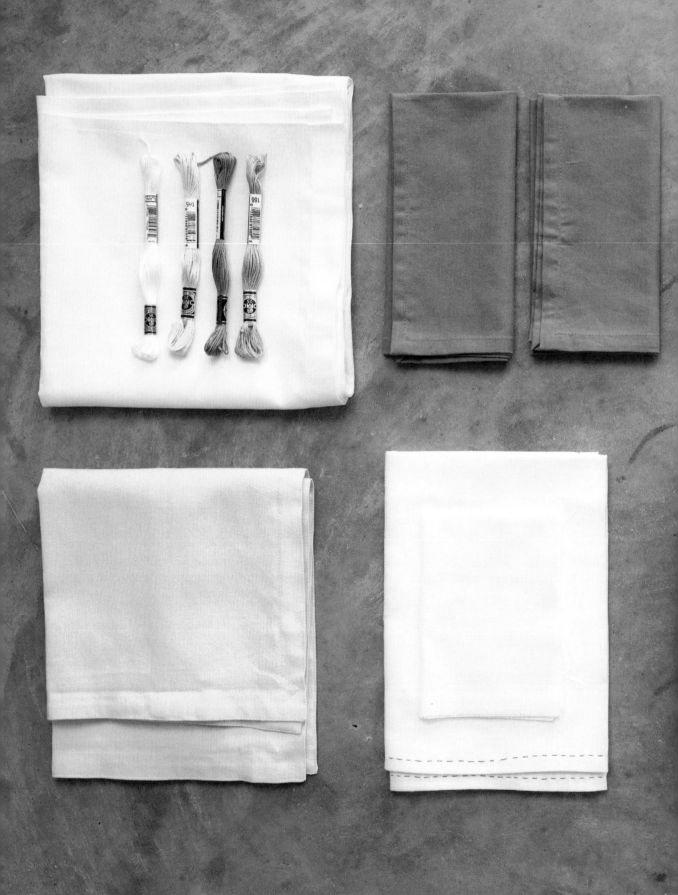

1. bold monogram napkins

see motifs on pages 38-39

working kitchen tablecloth

see motifs on pages 40-41

3. best wish bottle cozy

see motifs on pages 42-43

peace

see motifs on pages 42-43

4. peace and love sampler

5. say it with symbols

see motifs on pages 44-45

pop

6. bright idea journal cover

see motifs on pages 44-45

7. **on-the-go snack sack**

see motifs on page 46

8. flower power curtains

see motifs on page 47

9. sitting pretty stool cover

see motifs on pages 48-49

see motifs on page 50

10. berry cozy throw

11. bird blouse

see motifs on page 50

12. bikini keeper

see motifs on page 51

see motifs on pages 52-53

13. fresh greens throw pillows

14. blooming floor cushion

see motifs on pages 54-55

15. forest shade

see motifs on page 56

16. cut fruit
dishtowels

see motifs on page 57

17· forager's harvest tote

see motifs on pages 58-59

18. fun and games gift bag

see motifs on pages 58-59

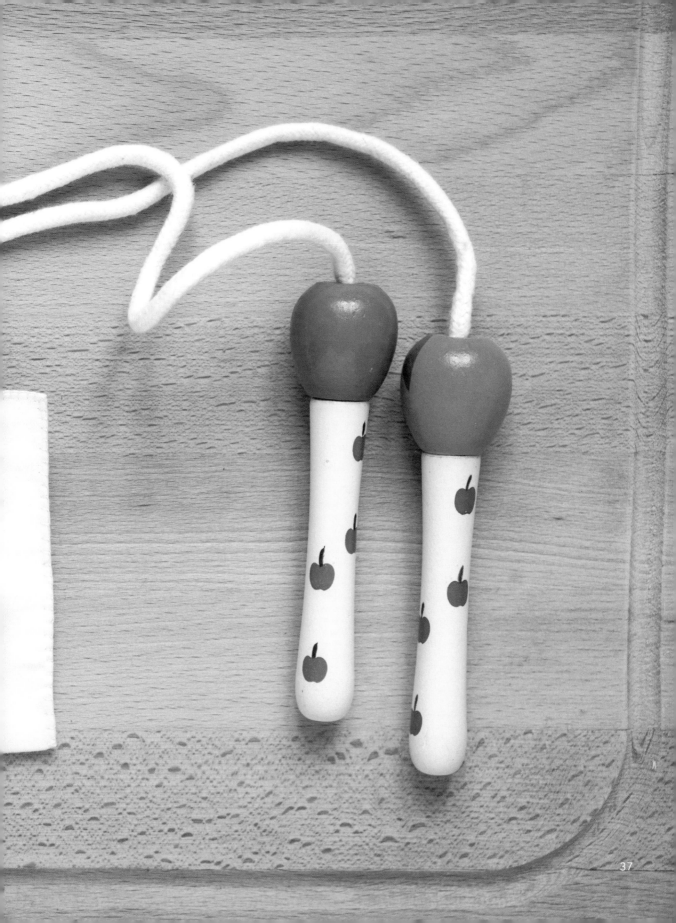

green motifs

see project on page 18

All the letters are filled in using rows of stem stitches side by side.

2. a well-stocked kitchen

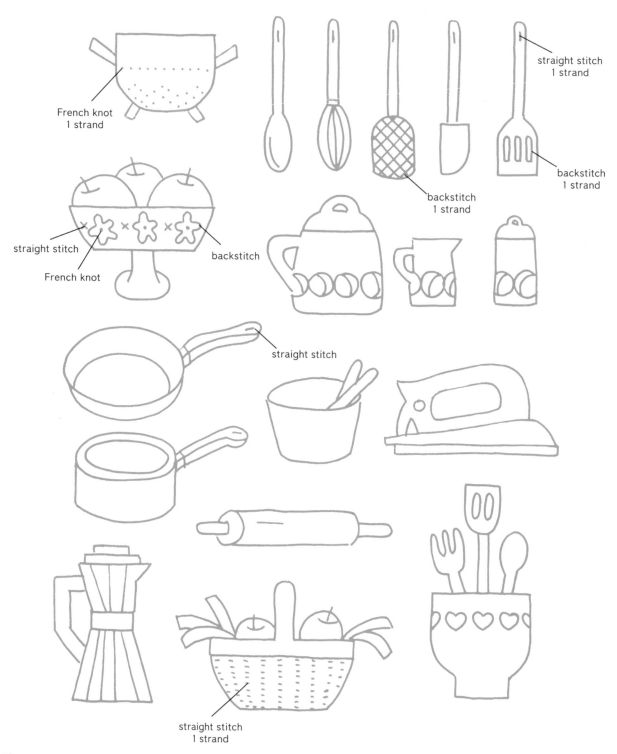

straight stitch
1 strand

French knot
1 strand

backstitch
1 strand

backstitch
1 strand

straight stitch

French knot

backstitch

straight stitch

straight stitch
1 strand

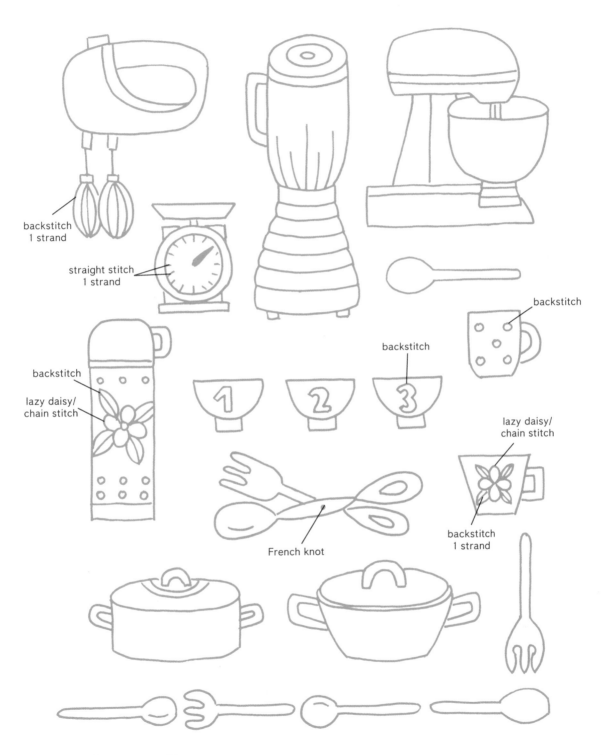

backstitch
1 strand

straight stitch
1 strand

backstitch

backstitch

backstitch

backstitch

lazy daisy/
chain stitch

lazy daisy/
chain stitch

backstitch
1 strand

French knot

see project on page 19

peace and love aplenty

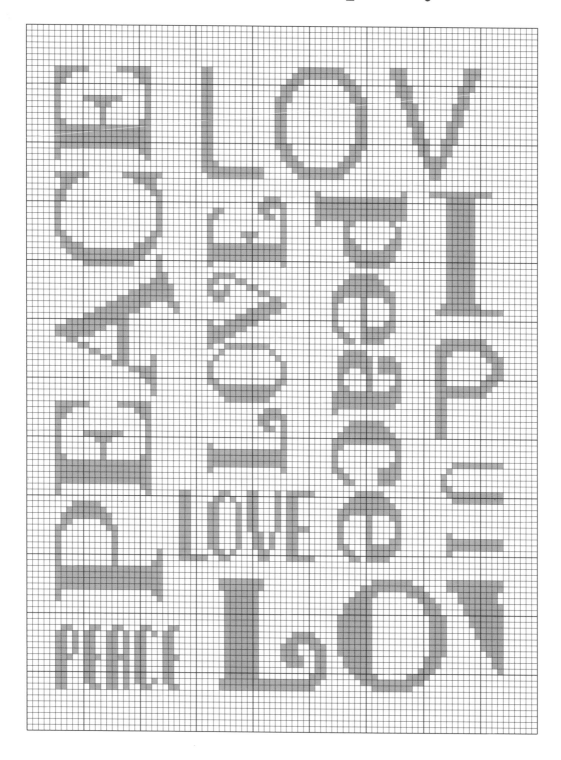

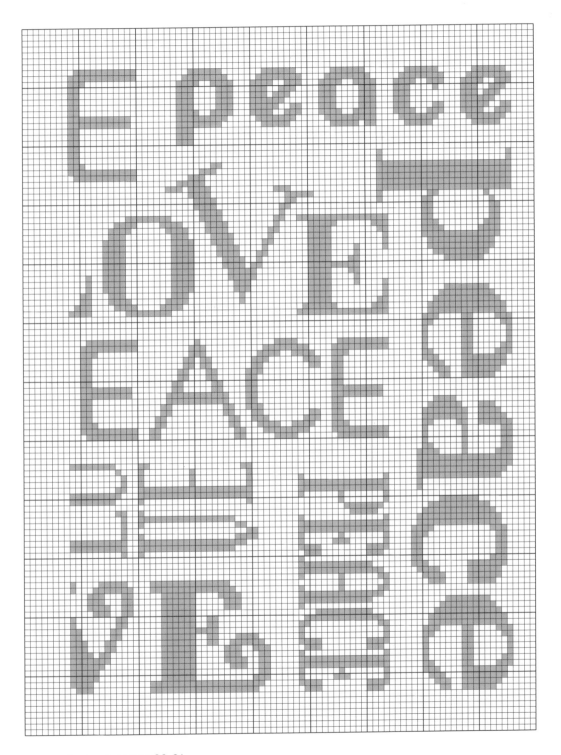

see projects on pages 20-21

no words needed

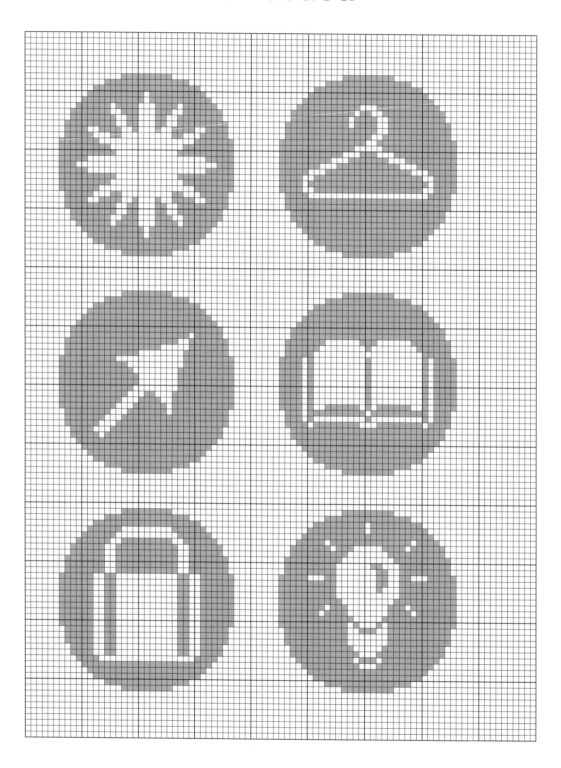

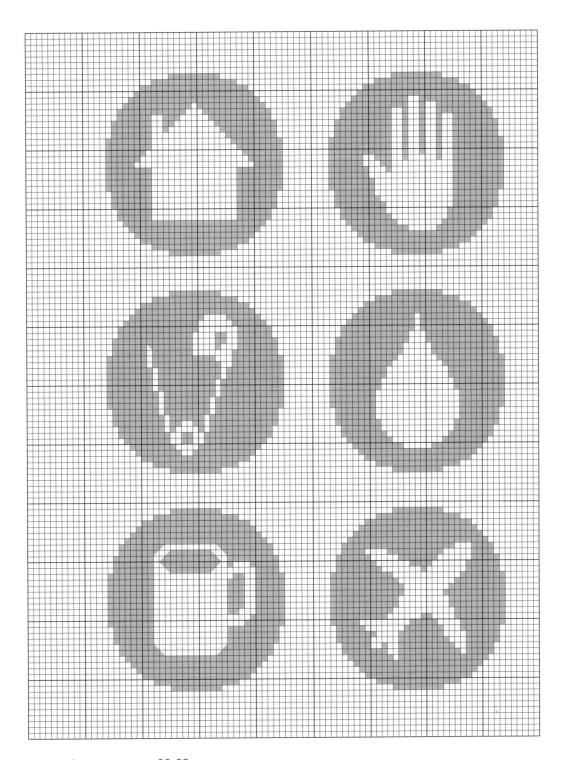

see projects on pages 22-23

see project on page 24

see project on page 25

9. fanciful blooms

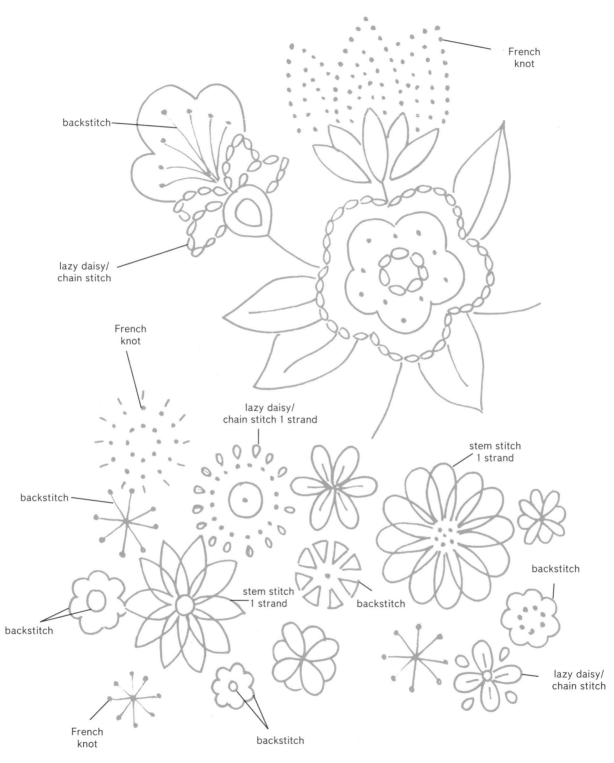

French knot

backstitch

lazy daisy/ chain stitch

French knot

lazy daisy/ chain stitch 1 strand

stem stitch 1 strand

backstitch

backstitch

stem stitch 1 strand

backstitch

backstitch

backstitch

lazy daisy/ chain stitch

French knot

backstitch

48

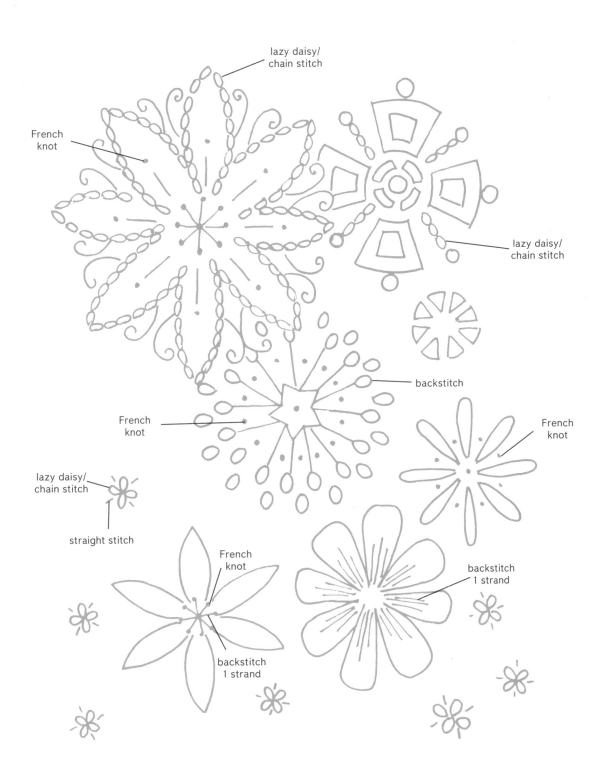

lazy daisy/
chain stitch

French
knot

lazy daisy/
chain stitch

backstitch

French
knot

French
knot

lazy daisy/
chain stitch

straight stitch

French
knot

backstitch
1 strand

backstitch
1 strand

see project on page 26

10 & 11. birds and berries

French knot
1 strand

straight stitch

backstitch

lazy daisy/
chain stitch

French
knot

French knot
1 strand

see projects on pages 27-28

see project on page 29

13. stylish trees

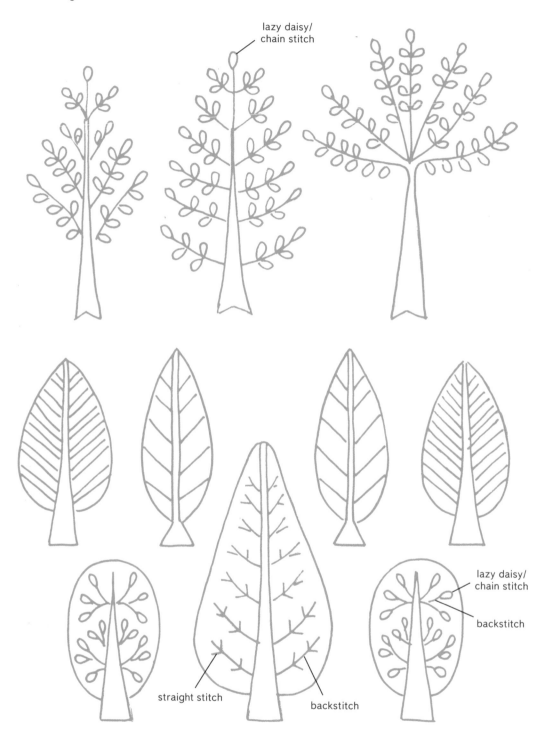

lazy daisy/
chain stitch

lazy daisy/
chain stitch

backstitch

straight stitch

backstitch

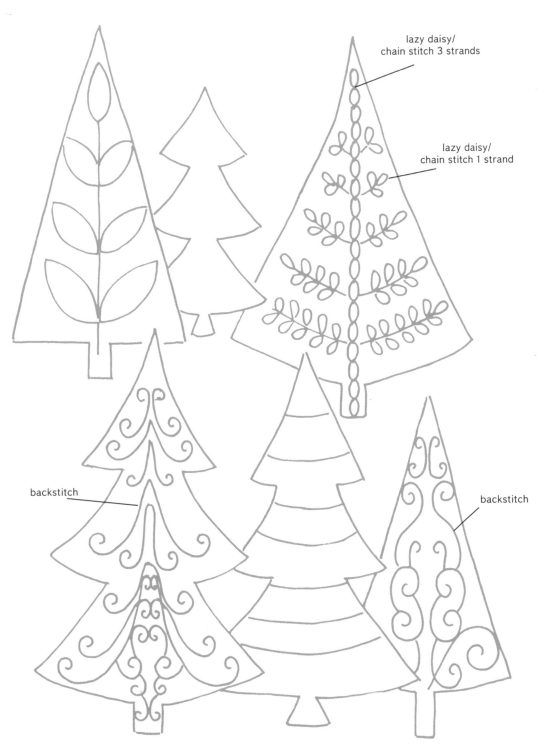

lazy daisy/
chain stitch 3 strands

lazy daisy/
chain stitch 1 strand

backstitch

backstitch

see project on pages 30-31

14. simple seeds and pods

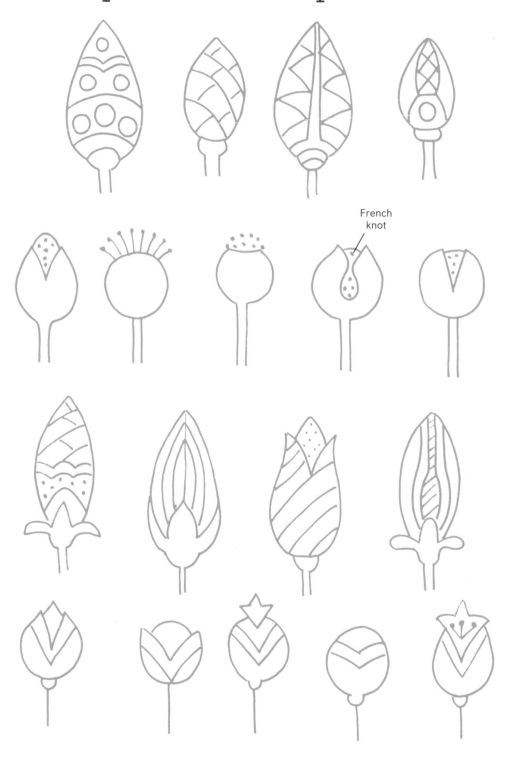

French knot

French
knot

see project on page 32

15. forest friends

see project on page 33

apples and pears

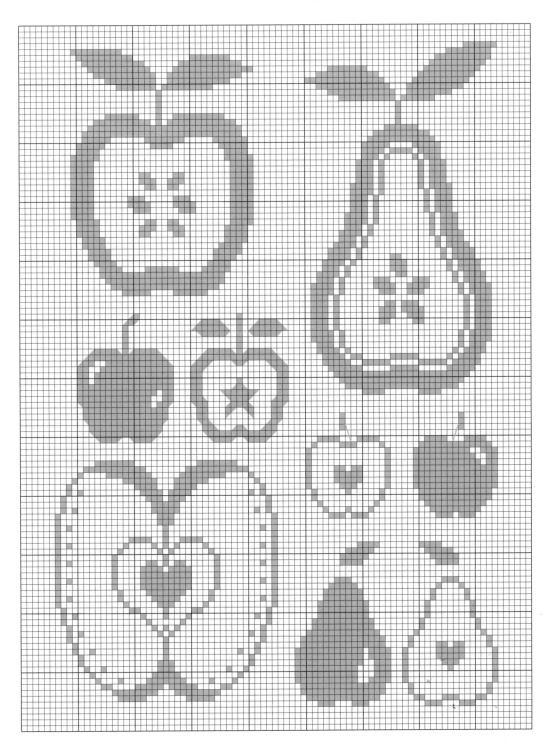

see project on page 34

17 & 18. fun at the park

lazy daisy/
chain stitch

straight stitch
1 strand

lazy daisy/
chain stitch

straight
stitch

lazy daisy/
chain stitch 1 strand

French
knot

lazy daisy/
chain stitch

French knot
1 strand

backstitch

French
knot

lazy daisy/
chain stitch

straight stitch

French
knot

lazy daisy/
chain stitch

lazy daisy/
chain stitch

straight stitch

French
knot

French
knot

straight
stitch

see projects on pages 35-36

pink

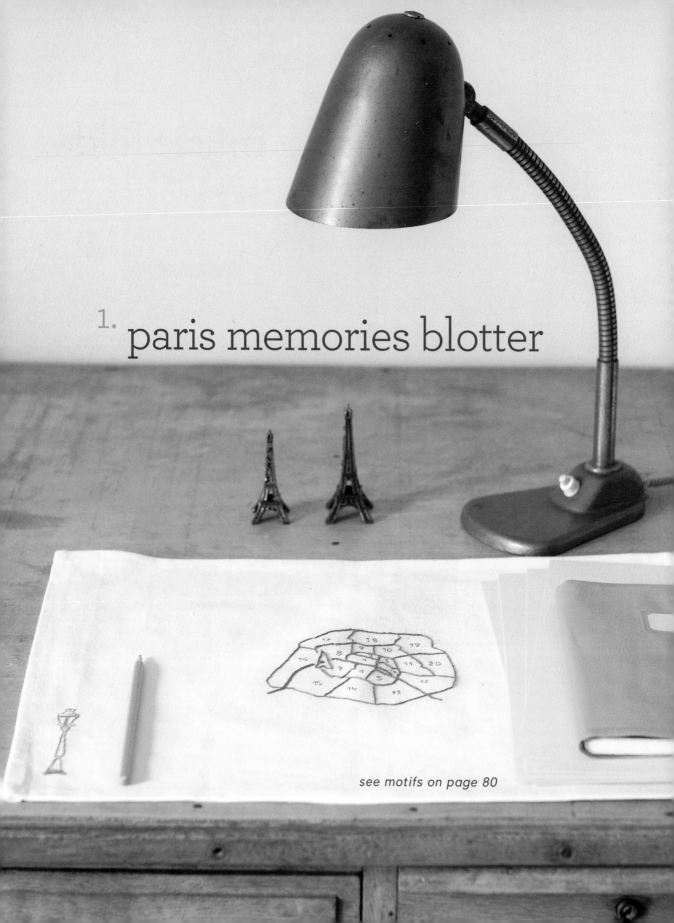

1. paris memories blotter

see motifs on page 80

2. sheet music folder

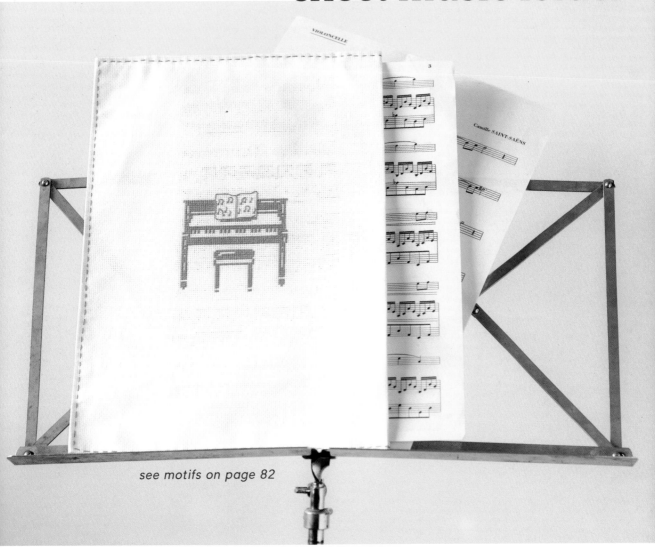

see motifs on page 82

RUE
DE LA PAIX

3. shade with a view

see motifs on page 81

4. pretty in pink slippers

see motifs on page 83

5. samplers with a french twist

I LOVE PARIS

PinK

ABCD
EFG HI
JKLMN
OPQ
RST UV
WXYZ

see motifs on page 84-87

ABCDEFGHI
JKLMNOPQR
STUVWXYZ
abcdefghijklm
nopqrstuvwxyz

ROSE

6. garden patio tablecloth

see motifs on page 88

7. pretty bird napkins

see motifs on page 89

8. lovebirds sachet

see motifs on page 90

see motifs on page 91

9. cozy cats cushion

10. lingerie travel bag

see motifs on page 92

11. chic ladies scarf

see motifs on pages 94-95

12. just desserts chair cover

see motifs on page 93

13. pink poodles runner

see motifs on page 96

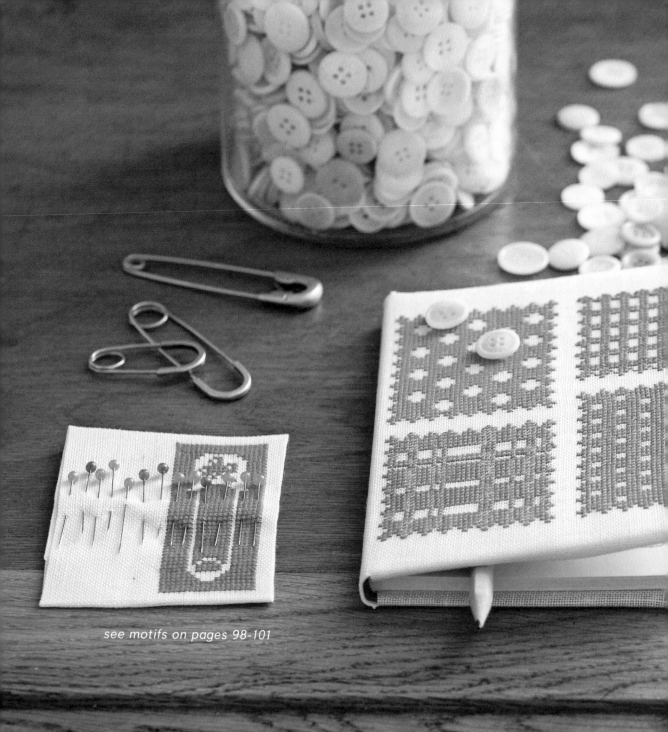

see motifs on pages 98-101

76

14. sewing room accessories

15. secret diary

see motifs on page 97

16. sidewalk café shopping bag

see motifs on pages 102-103

pink motifs

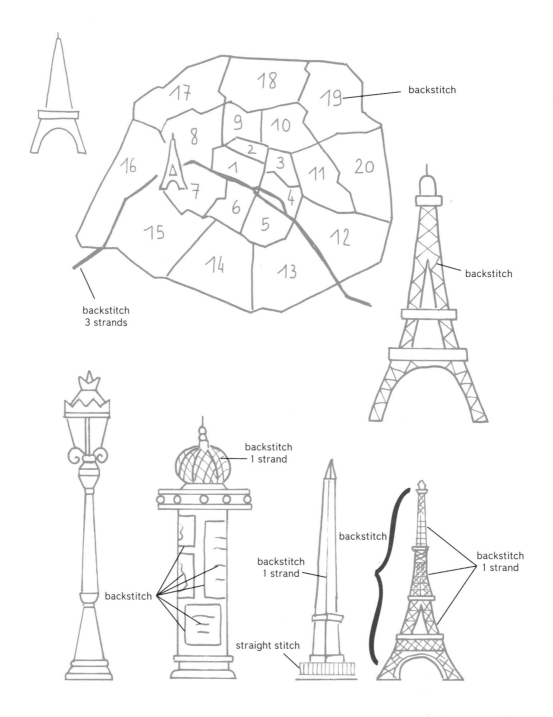

backstitch

backstitch

backstitch
3 strands

backstitch
1 strand

backstitch

backstitch

backstitch
1 strand

backstitch
1 strand

straight stitch

see project on page 62

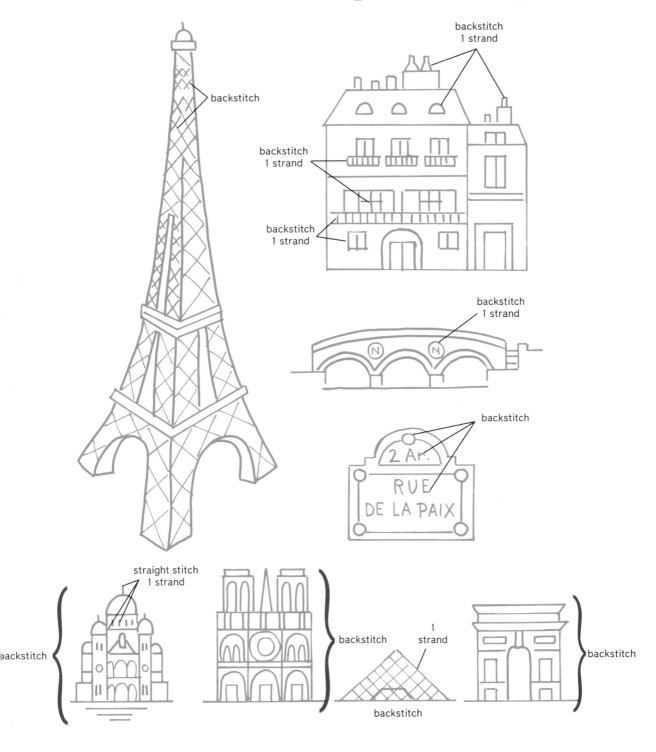

backstitch

backstitch
1 strand

backstitch
1 strand

backstitch
1 strand

backstitch
1 strand

backstitch

2 An.
RUE
DE LA PAIX

straight stitch
1 strand

backstitch

backstitch

1
strand

backstitch

backstitch

see project on page 64

2. musical instruments

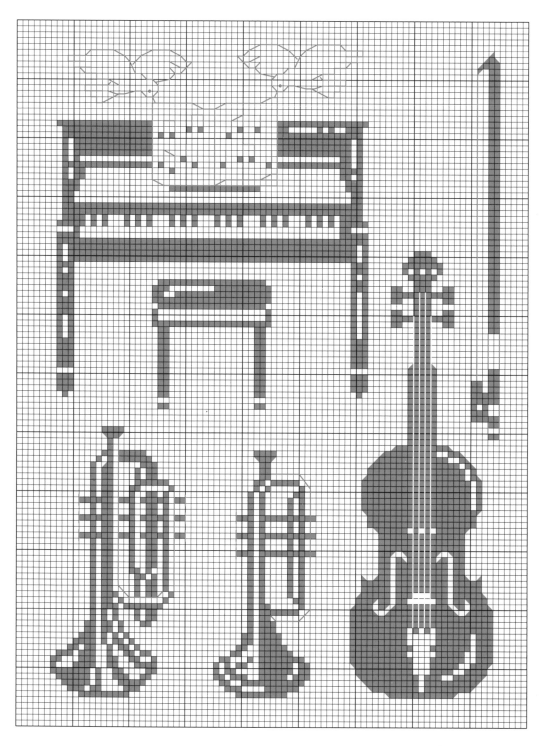

see project on page 63

4. scattered petals

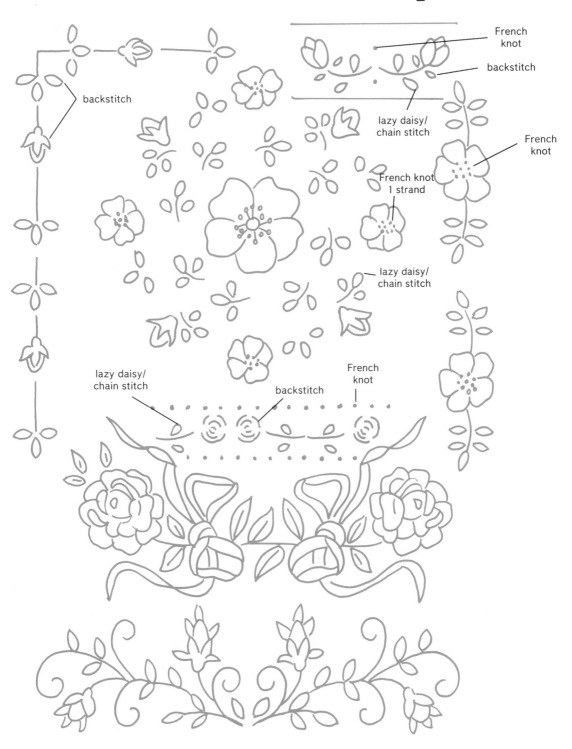

French knot

backstitch

backstitch

lazy daisy/
chain stitch

French knot

French knot
1 strand

lazy daisy/
chain stitch

lazy daisy/
chain stitch

backstitch

French knot

see project on page 65

5. art deco alphabets

see project on pages 66-67

art deco alphabets

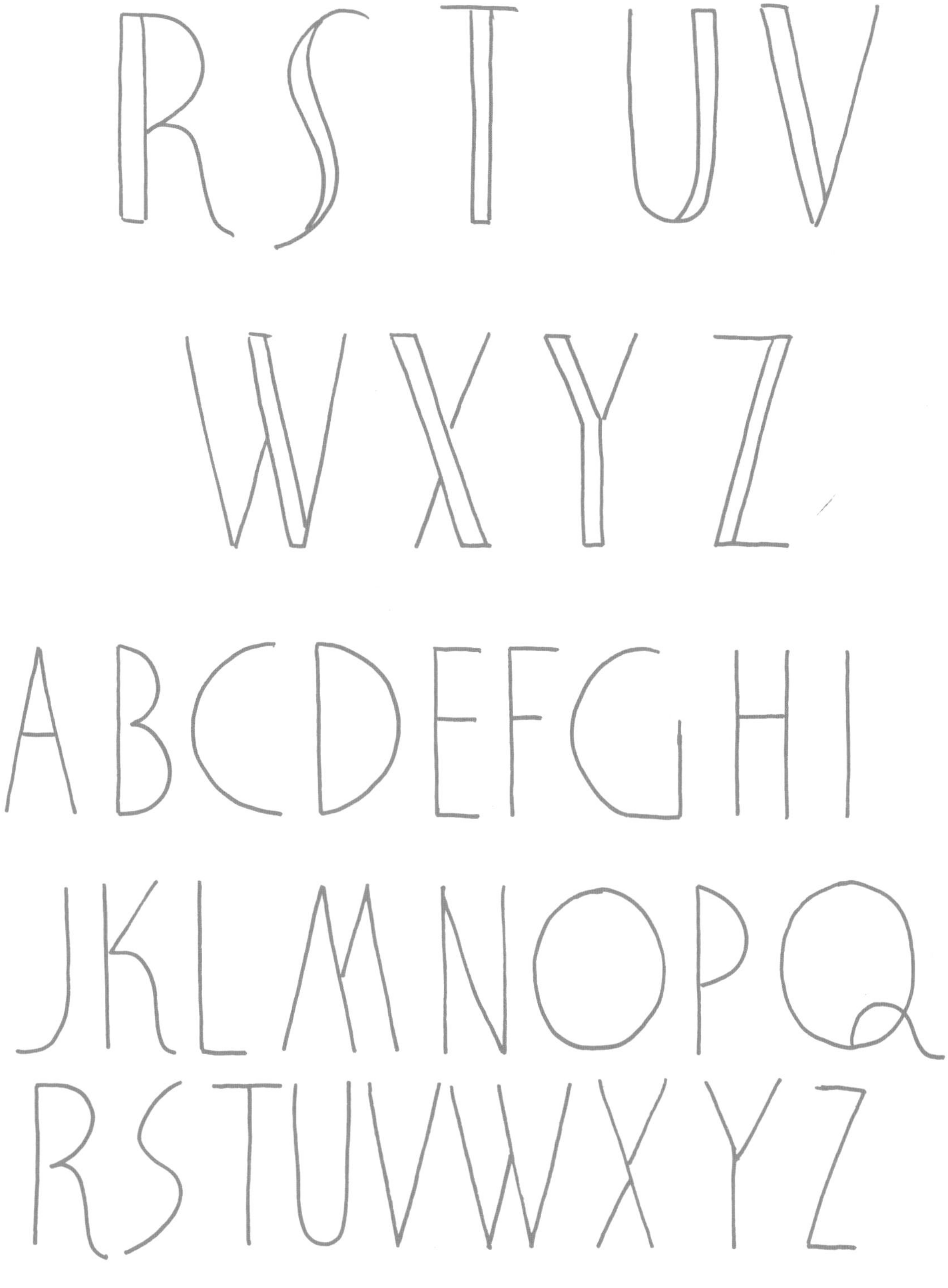

R S T U V

W X Y Z

A B C D E F G H I

J K L M N O P Q

R S T U V W X Y Z

see project on pages 66-67

6. in the garden

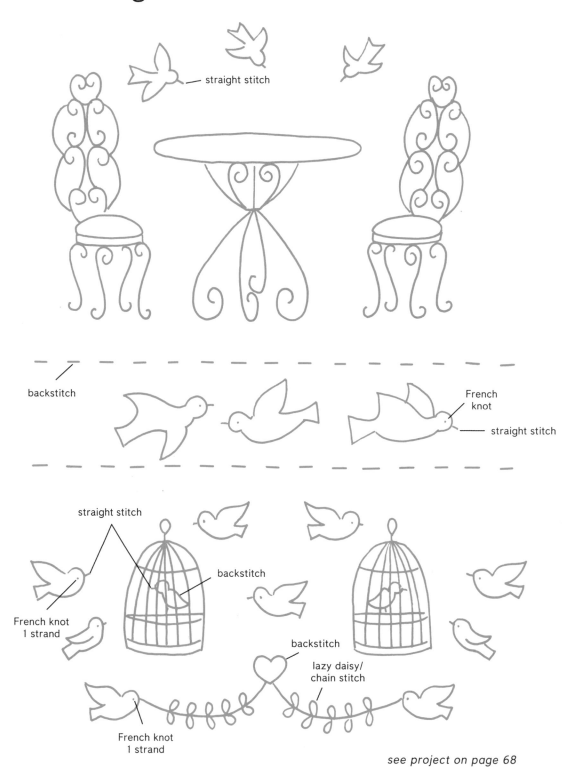

straight stitch

backstitch

French knot

straight stitch

straight stitch

backstitch

French knot
1 strand

backstitch

lazy daisy/
chain stitch

French knot
1 strand

see project on page 68

7. birds free and caged

see project on page 69

89

see project on page 70

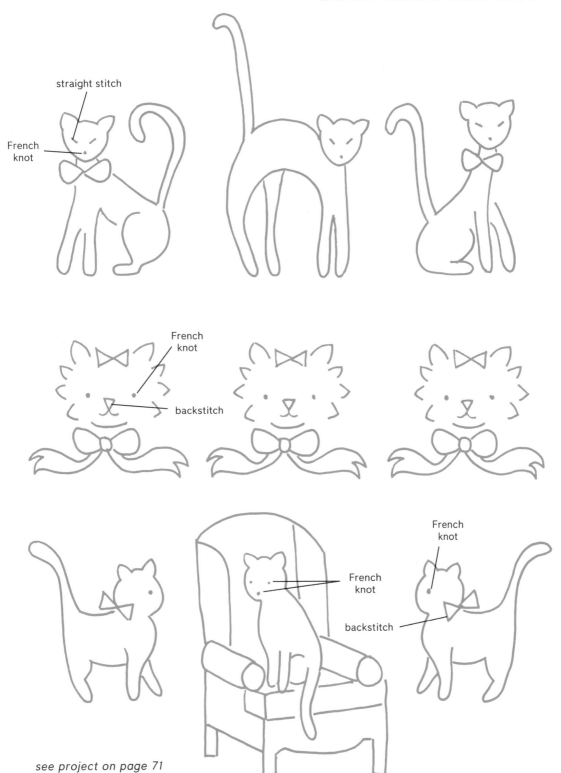

straight stitch

French knot

French knot

backstitch

French knot

French knot

backstitch

see project on page 71

10. packing for paris

backstitch
1 strand

French
knot

backstitch

backstitch

backstitch
1 strand

backstitch

French
knot

backstitch
1 strand

backstitch

French
knot

backstitch

straight stitch

see project on page 72

sweet shop

see project on page 74

classic french fashions

straight stitch

backstitch

backstitch

backstitch

straight stitch

straight stitch

lazy daisy/
chain stitch

straight stitch
1 strand

straight stitch
1 strand

backstitch

backstitch

French knot
1 strand

French
knot

straight stitch

French
knot

backstitch

straight stitch

see project on page 73

13. poodles promenade

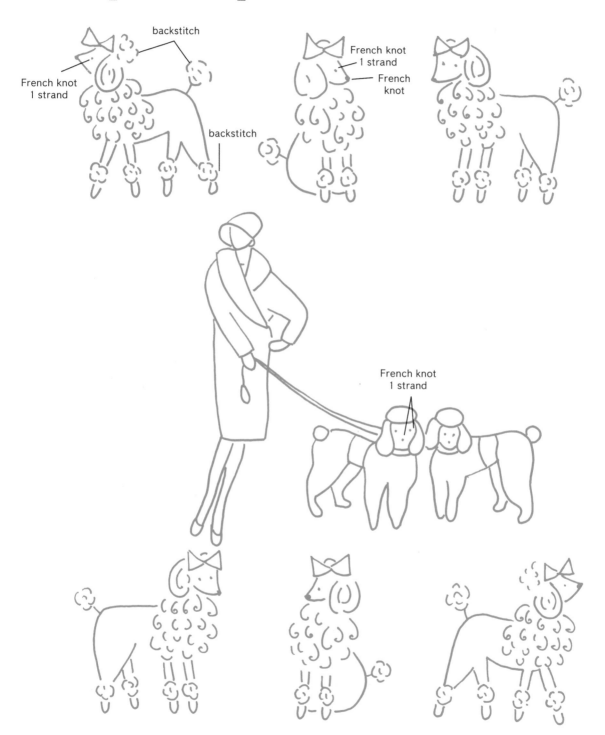

backstitch

French knot
1 strand

backstitch

French knot
1 strand

French knot

French knot
1 strand

see project on page 75

15. old fashioned parasols

see project on page 78

14. sewing box

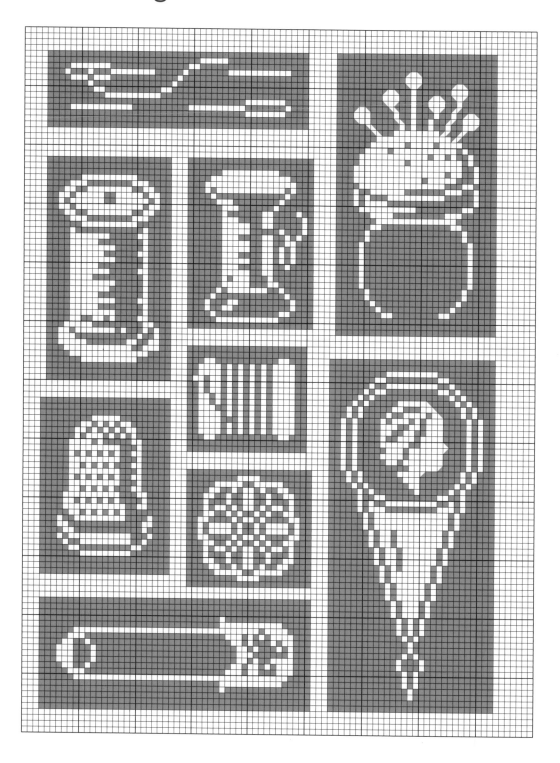

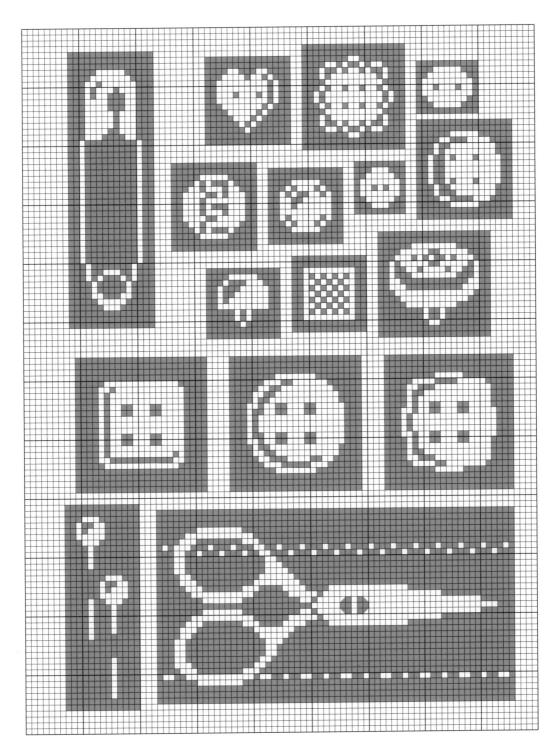

see project on pages 76-77

14. borders and patterns

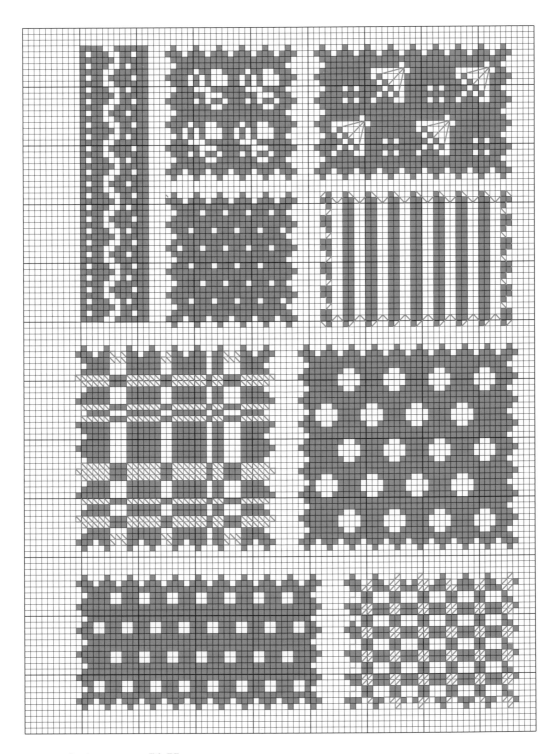

see project on pages 76-77

16. window shopping

backstitch

1

CAFE

French
knot

backstitch
1 strand

backstitch

backstitch

PARFUM

backstitch

back-
stitch

lazy daisy/
chain stitch

French
knot

backstitch

French
knot

backstitch
1 strand

see project on page 79

blue

custom converse

see motifs on pages 120-121

2. guardian angel sampler

see motifs on pages 120-121

3. writer's messenger bag

see motifs on pages 122-123

4. travel journals

see motifs on pages 124-125

5. bluebird ballet flats

see motifs on pages 126-127

BLEU

see motifs on pages 128-129

6. french blue dress

7. teatime tea towel

see motifs on pages 130-131

8. dutch blue napkins

see motifs on pages 132-133

9. fishy beach towel

see motifs on pages 134-135

10. sailor's knot beach bag

see motifs on pages 136-137

11. beach picnic sack

see motifs on pages 138-139

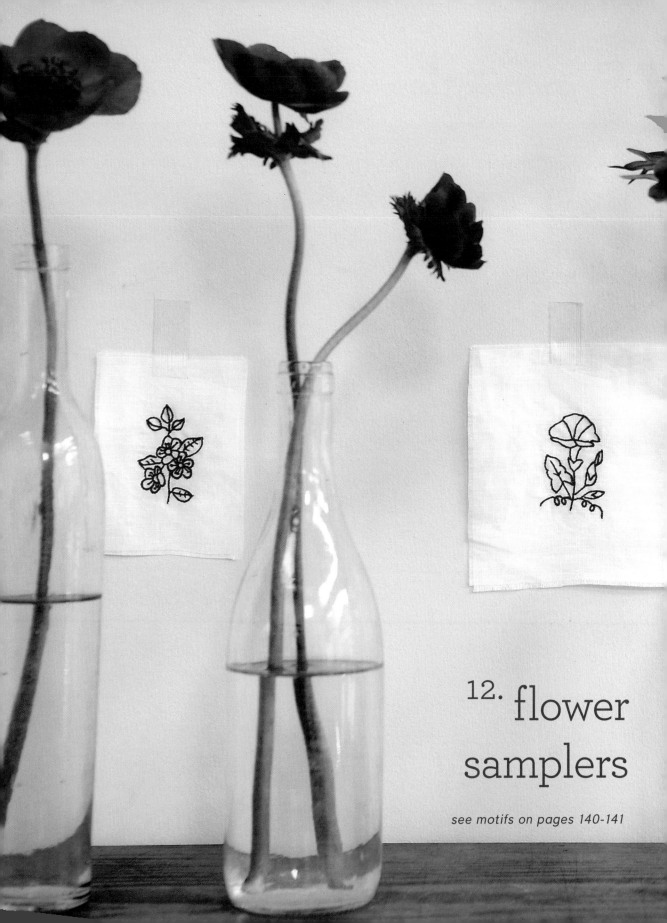

12. flower samplers

see motifs on pages 140-141

13. racer's tee

see motifs on pages 142-145

14. night serenade pillowcase

see motifs on pages 146-147

blue motifs

1 & 2. sampler and borders

see projects on pages 106-107

3. written by hand

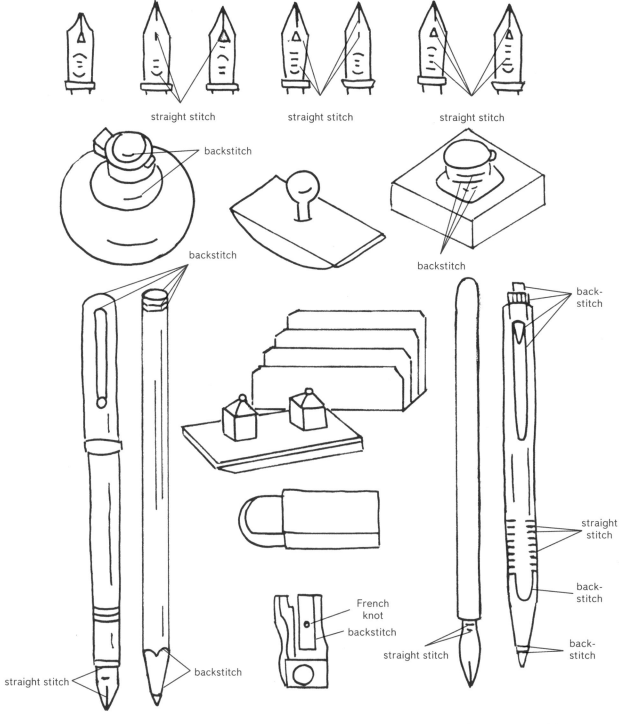

straight stitch   straight stitch   straight stitch

backstitch

backstitch

backstitch

backstitch

back-stitch

straight stitch

back-stitch

French knot
backstitch

straight stitch

straight stitch

back-stitch

straight stitch   backstitch

see project on page 108

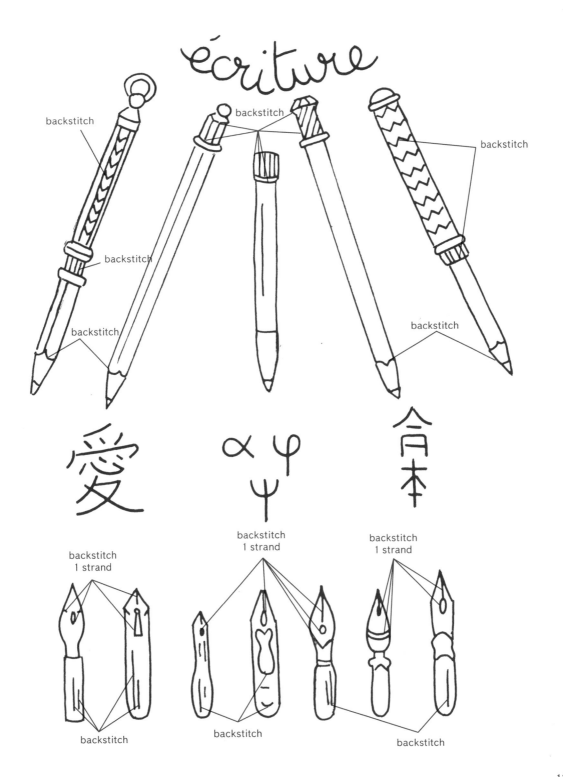

écriture

backstitch

backstitch

backstitch

backstitch

backstitch

backstitch

愛　αΨ　合
　　　Ψ　　本

backstitch
1 strand

backstitch
1 strand

backstitch
1 strand

backstitch

backstitch

backstitch

4· exotic florals

see project on page 109

5· birds in flight

straight stitch

straight stitch

French knot

straight stitch

backstitch

backstitch

backstitch

backstitch

French
knot

backstitch

straight stitch

lazy daisy/
chain stitch

backstitch

see project on page 110

6. art nouveau alphabet

backstitch

stem stitch
1 strand

backstitch

backstitch

stem stitch
1 strand

stem stitch
1 strand

stem stitch
1 strand

see project on page 111

7. coffee and tea

see project on page 112

8. tulips and windmills

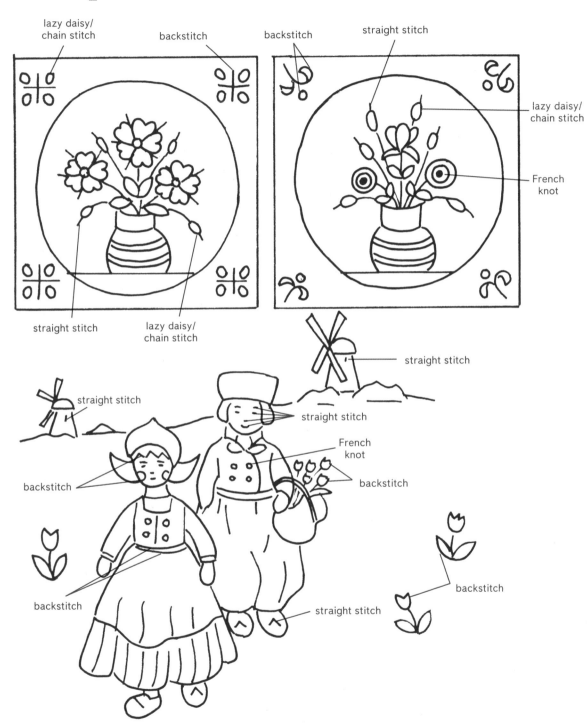

lazy daisy/
chain stitch

backstitch

backstitch

straight stitch

lazy daisy/
chain stitch

French
knot

straight stitch

lazy daisy/
chain stitch

straight stitch

straight stitch

straight stitch

backstitch

French
knot

backstitch

backstitch

backstitch

straight stitch

straight stitch

backstitch

backstitch

French knot

straight stitch

backstitch 1 strand

backstitch

backstitch

backstitch 1 strand

straight stitch

backstitch

backstitch

backstitch

see project on page 113

9. deep blue sea

see project on page 114

^{10.} mariner's landing

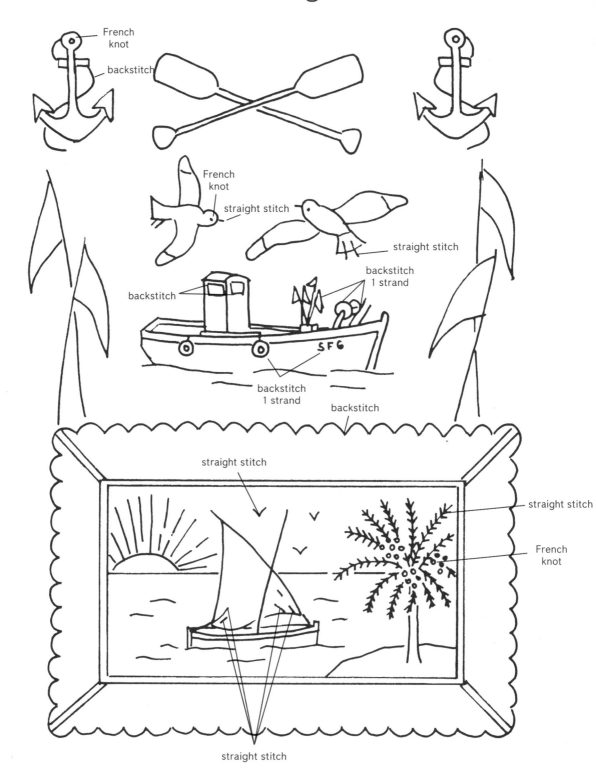

French knot
backstitch
French knot
straight stitch
straight stitch
backstitch 1 strand
backstitch
backstitch 1 strand
SF6
backstitch
straight stitch
straight stitch
French knot
straight stitch

backstitch

see project on page 115

day at the beach

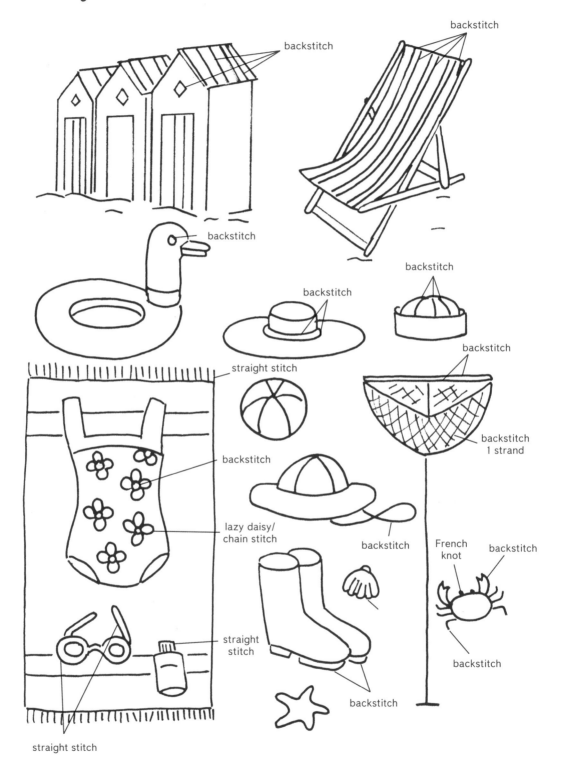

backstitch

backstitch

backstitch

backstitch

backstitch

backstitch

straight stitch

backstitch

backstitch
1 strand

backstitch

lazy daisy/
chain stitch

French
knot

backstitch

backstitch

straight
stitch

backstitch

backstitch

straight stitch

backstitch

backstitch   backstitch

backstitch   backstitch   backstitch

backstitch

backstitch

backstitch

straight
stitch

straight
stitch

straight stitch

backstitch

backstitch

see project on page 116

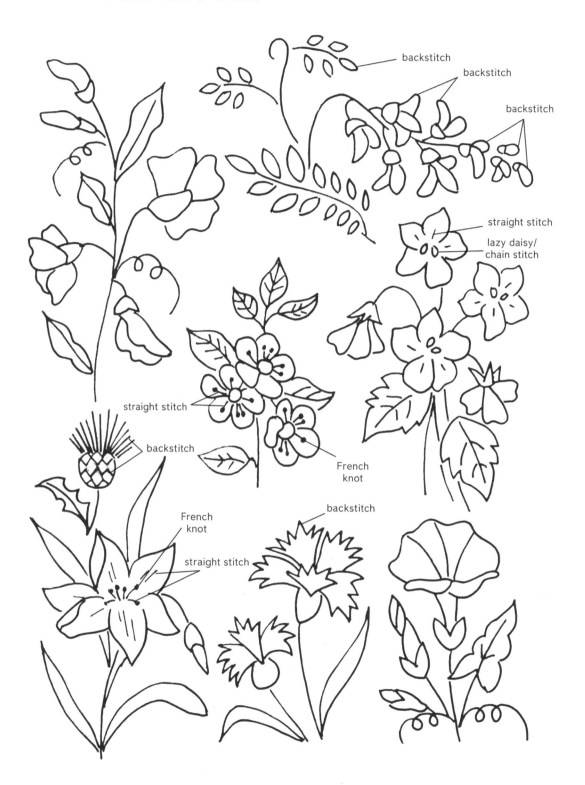

backstitch

backstitch

backstitch

straight stitch

lazy daisy/
chain stitch

straight stitch

backstitch

French
knot

French
knot

backstitch

straight stitch

French
knot

French
knot

straight stitch

French
knot

see project on page 117

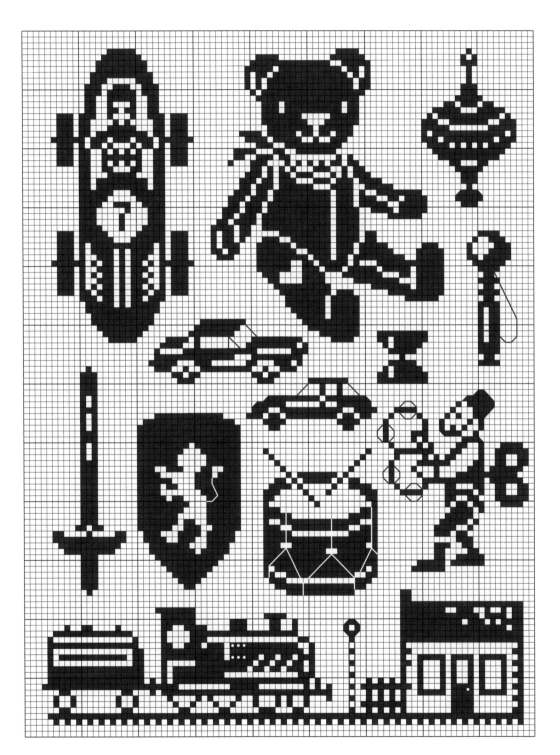

see project on page 118

¹³· more kids' stuff

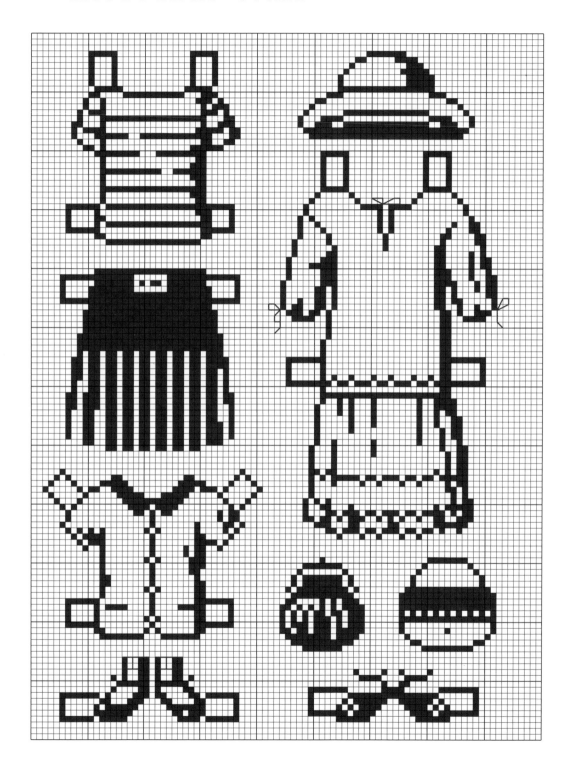

144

14· night skies

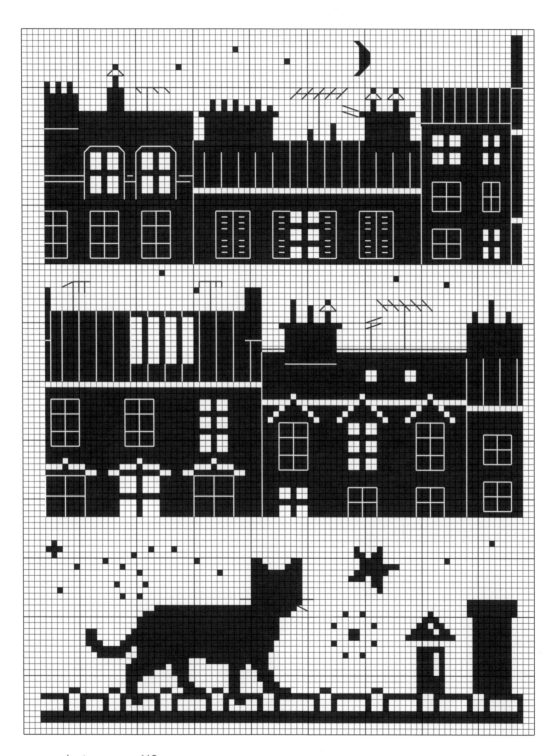

see project on page 119

red

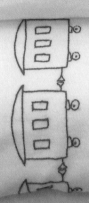

1. choo-choo dreams

see motifs on pages 168-169

see motifs on page 170

2. a little doll's dress

4. frolicking angels picnic blanket

see motifs on pages 172-173

5. gardener's apron

see motifs on page 174

6. antique roses tablecloth

see motifs on page 175

see motifs on pages 176-177

8. country walk table runner

see motifs on page 178

9. rainy day book bag

see motifs on page 179

10. chef's notebook

see motifs on page 180

11. summer's day
dishtowel

see motifs on page 181

12. let it snow bath towels

see motifs on pages 182-183

13. classic coverlet

see motifs on pages 184-185

see motifs on pages 186-187

164

see motifs on page 191

15. love and blessings
bedlinens

16. monogrammed sampler

see motifs on page 190

17. stitched santa ornament

see motifs on pages 188-189

red motifs

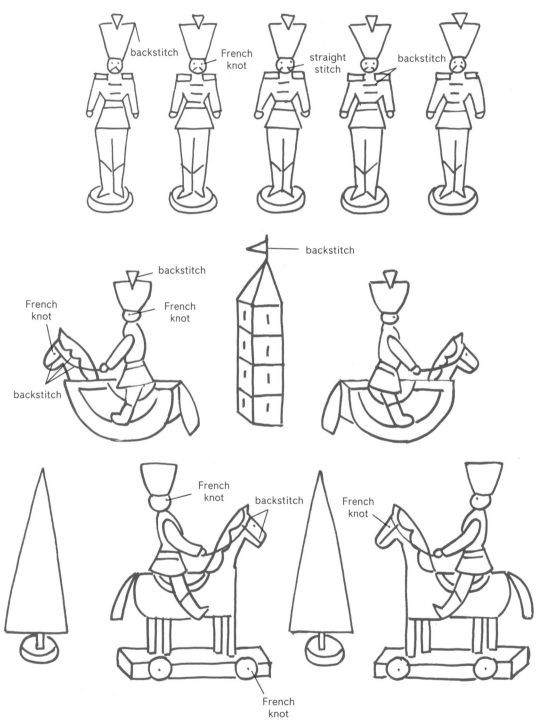

backstitch

French knot

straight stitch

backstitch

backstitch

French knot

French knot

backstitch

backstitch

French knot

backstitch

French knot

French knot

backstitch

French knot

French knot

see project on page 150

1. toys on wheels

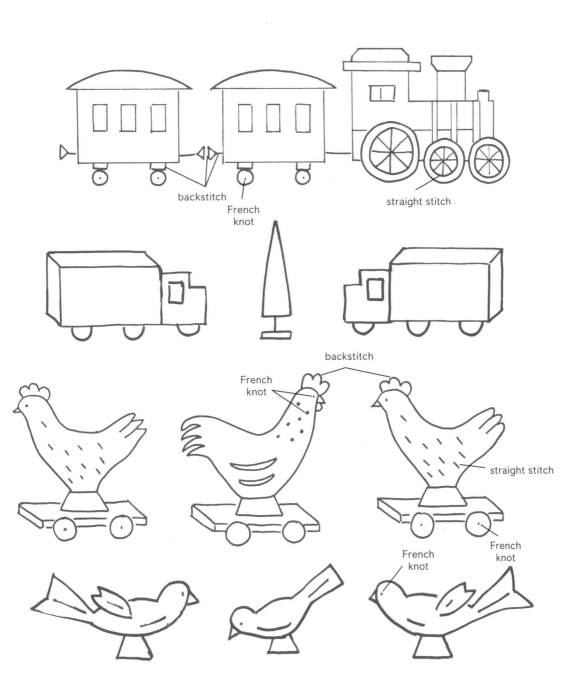

backstitch

French knot

straight stitch

backstitch

French knot

straight stitch

French knot

French knot

2. dolls and teddies

French knot

backstitch

backstitch

backstitch

backstitch

backstitch

backstitch

backstitch

front

see project on page 151

3. red poppies

see project on page 152

4. angels

see project on page 153

5. garden visitors

straight stitch

French knot

lazy daisy/ chain stitch

straight stitch

French knot

backstitch

backstitch

straight stitch

French knot

French knot

backstitch

French knot

French knot

French knot

French knot

straight stitch

backstitch

straight stitch

see project on page 154

6. antique rose bouquet

lazy daisy/
chain stitch

straight stitch

backstitch

see project on page 155

7. continental christmas

see project on pages 156-157

8. girl tending geese

French knot

backstitch

lazy daisy/
chain stitch

backstitch

French
knot

backstitch

backstitch

backstitch

see project on page 158

9. a walk in the rain

straight stitch

French knot

straight stitch

backstitch

French knot

backstitch

straight stitch

see project on page 159

10. berries and pie

see project on page 160

11. insects and fish

see project on page 161

12. snowflakes

see project on page 162

13. classic borders

see project on page 163

14. hearts

see project on page 164

17. santas and christmas cheer

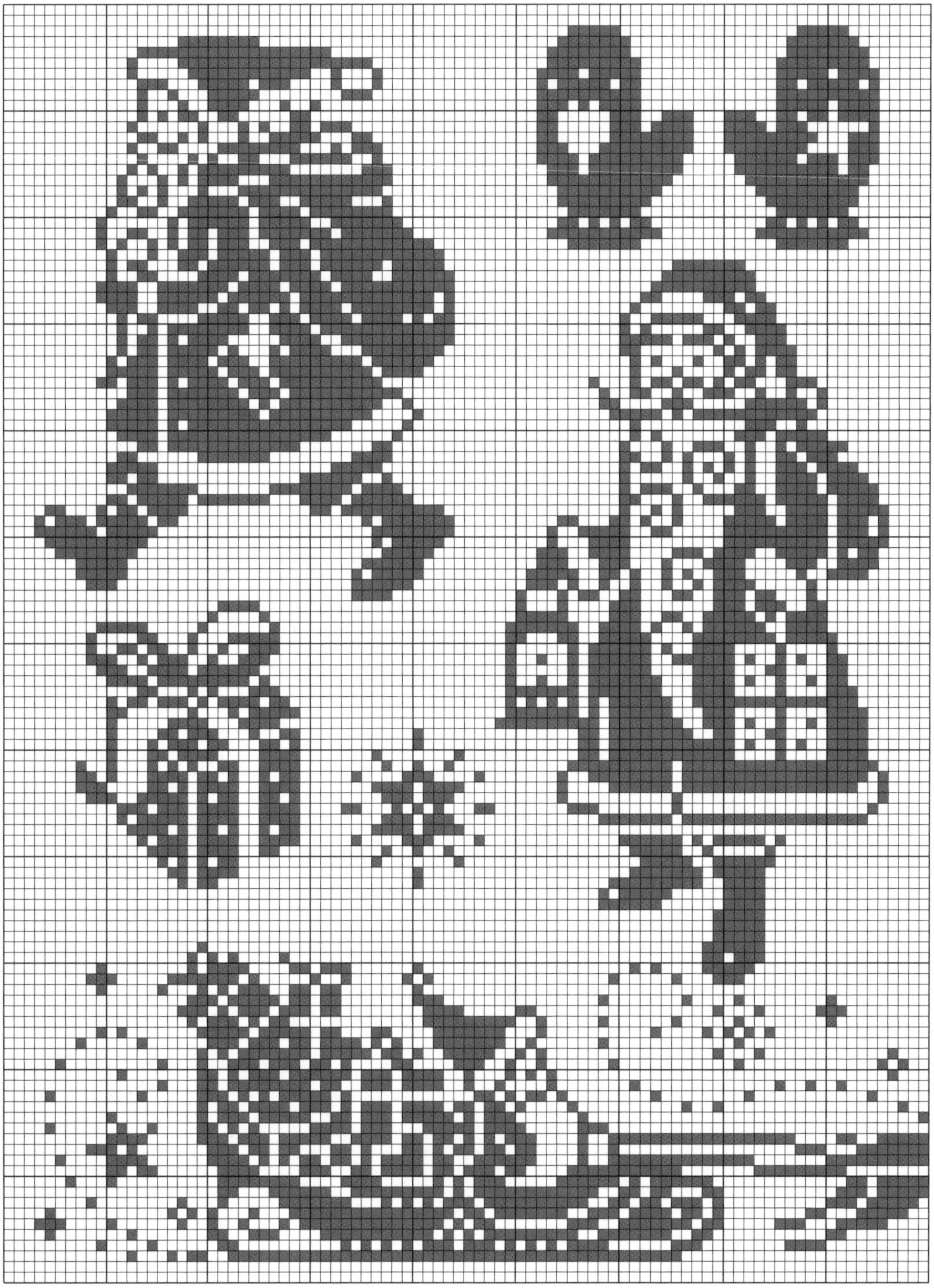

see project on page 167

16. monogrammed sampler

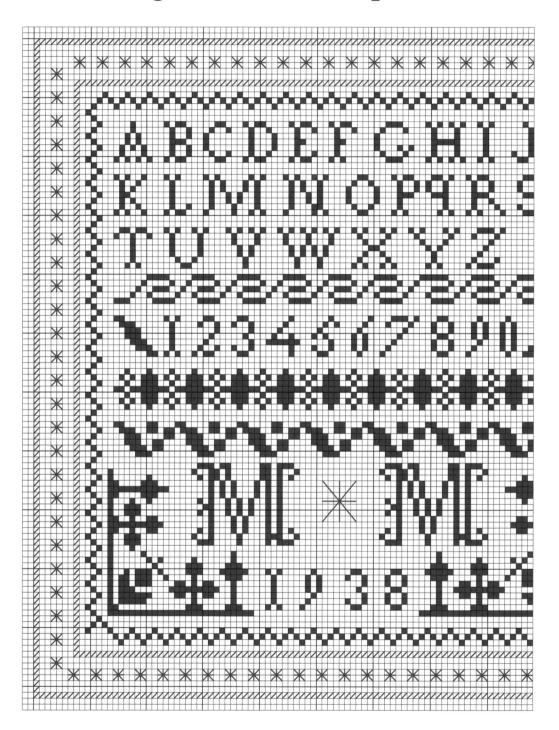

see project on page 166

15. angels and hearts

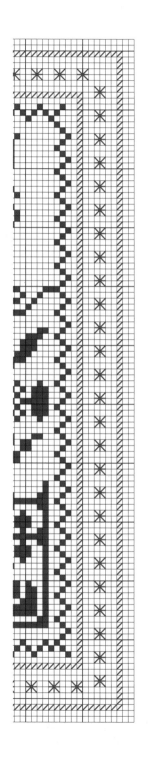

backstitch

backstitch

straight stitch

see project on page 165

white

1. wedding monogram

see motifs on pages 212-215

see motifs on pages 214-215

2. decorative pot cover

3. housewarming pillow

see motifs on page 216

see motifs on pages 217-218

4. stitcher's gift set

see motifs on page 219

5. framed portraits

6. cameo jacket

see motifs on page 220

7. summer breeze scarf

see motifs on page 221

8. inner light lampshade

see motifs on page 222

9· bird of peace clutch

see motifs on page 223

10. elegant monogrammed napkins

see motifs on pages 224-225

11. special day apron

see motifs on pages 226-227

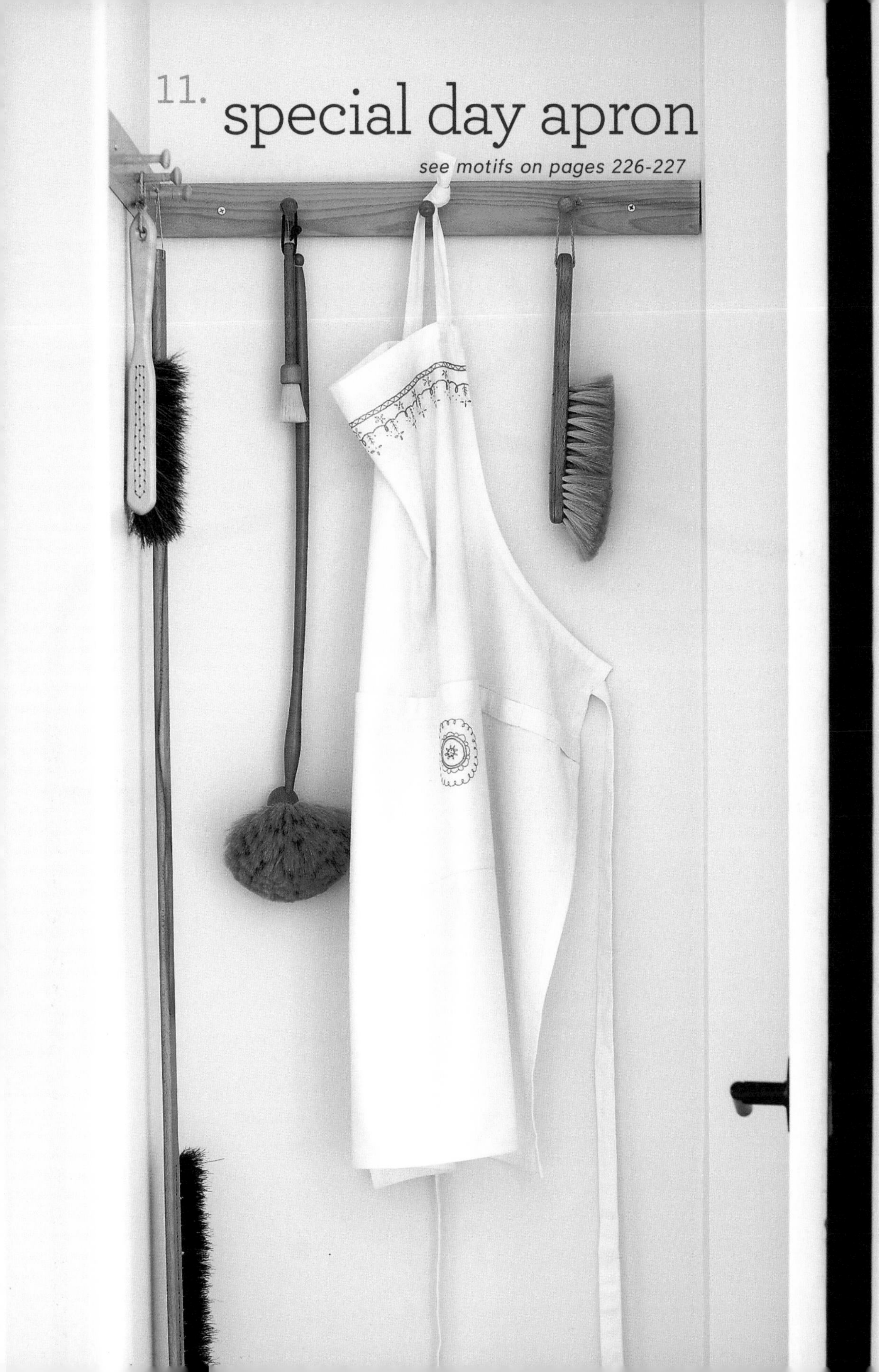

12. whimsical bath towels

see motifs on pages 228-229

13. sea and sand placemats

see motifs on pages 230-231

14. lace-stitched pillowcase

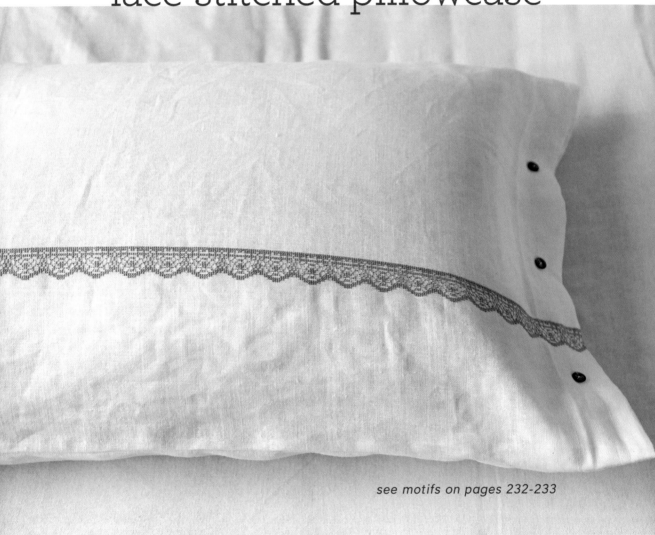

see motifs on pages 232-233

15. jam jar gift toppers

see motifs on pages 234-235

sketchpad cover

see motifs on page 236-237

see motifs on pages 232-233

17. embellished bottle vases

white motifs

see project on page 194

1 & 2. romantic alphabet

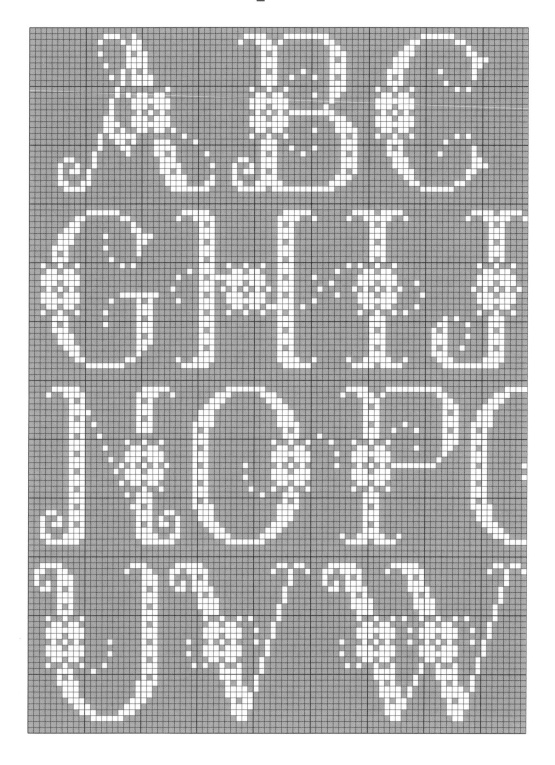

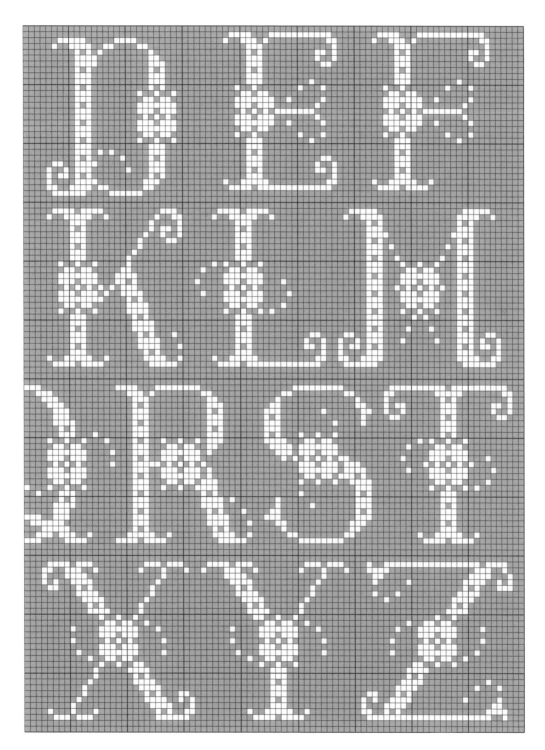

see projects on pages 194-195

3. good luck charms

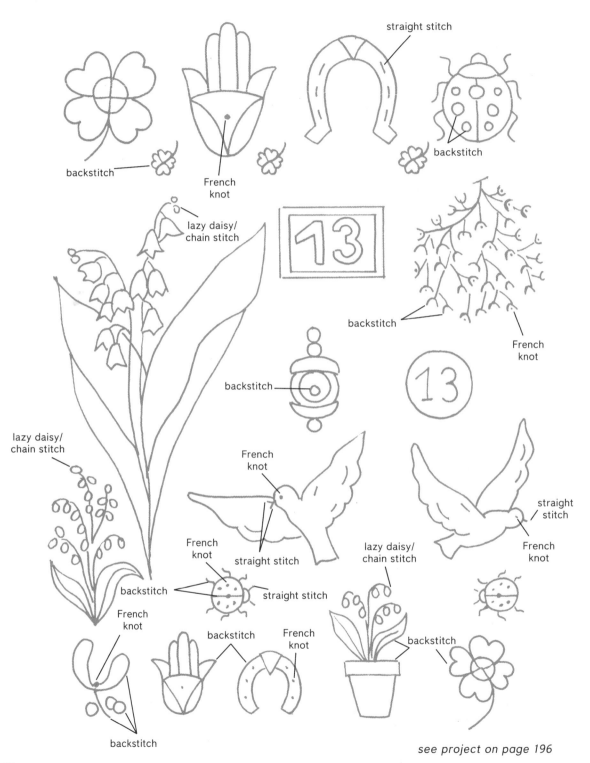

backstitch

straight stitch

backstitch

French
knot

lazy daisy/
chain stitch

backstitch

French
knot

lazy daisy/
chain stitch

backstitch

French
knot

straight
stitch

French
knot

French
knot

straight stitch

French
knot

lazy daisy/
chain stitch

backstitch

straight stitch

backstitch

French
knot

backstitch

backstitch

see project on page 196

see project on page 197

see project on page 197

see project on page 198-199

6. busts and cameos

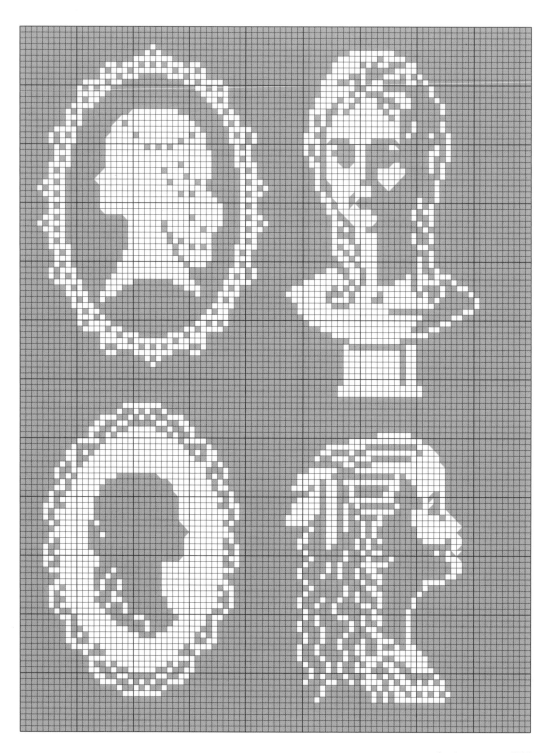

see project on page 200

7. garlands of flowers

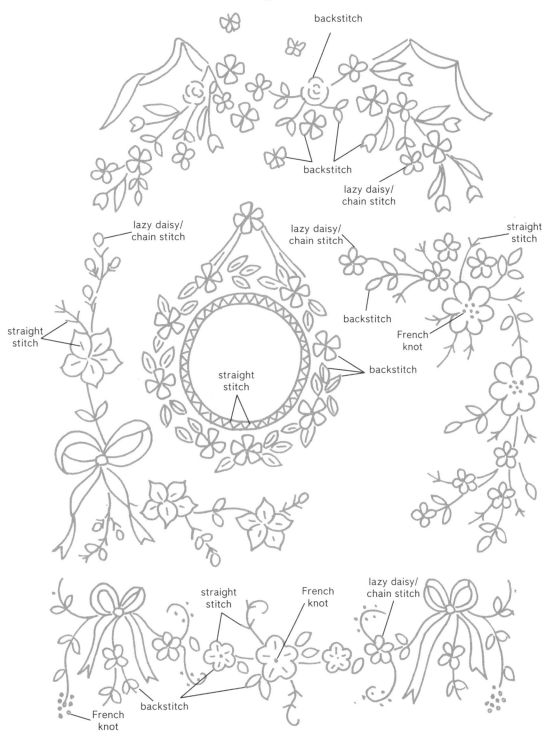

backstitch

backstitch

lazy daisy/
chain stitch

lazy daisy/
chain stitch

lazy daisy/
chain stitch

straight
stitch

backstitch

straight
stitch

straight
stitch

backstitch

French
knot

backstitch

straight
stitch

French
knot

lazy daisy/
chain stitch

backstitch

French
knot

see project on page 201

8. angels on high

backstitch

lazy daisy/
chain stitch

French
knot

straight stitch

French
knot

backstitch

lazy daisy/
chain stitch

French
knot

straight stitch

French
knot

straight stitch

see project on page 202

9. doves, cats, and a mouse

see project on page 203

10. flowery letters

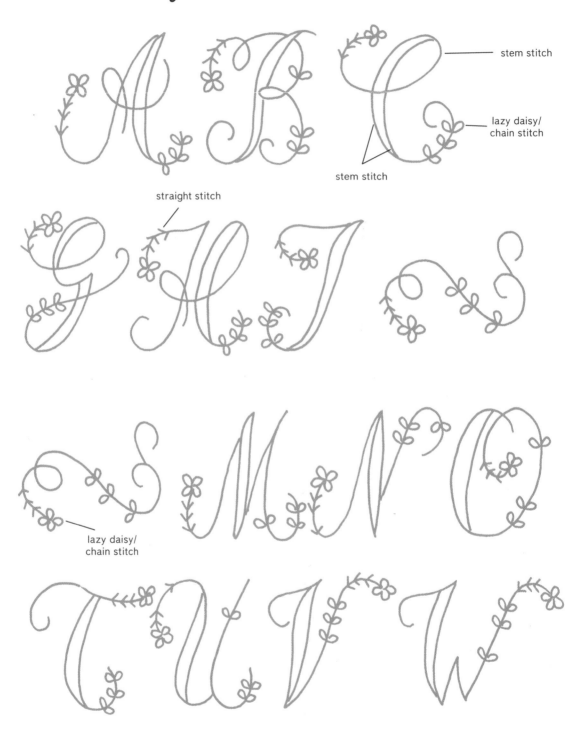

stem stitch

lazy daisy/
chain stitch

stem stitch

straight stitch

lazy daisy/
chain stitch

see project on page 204

vines and borders

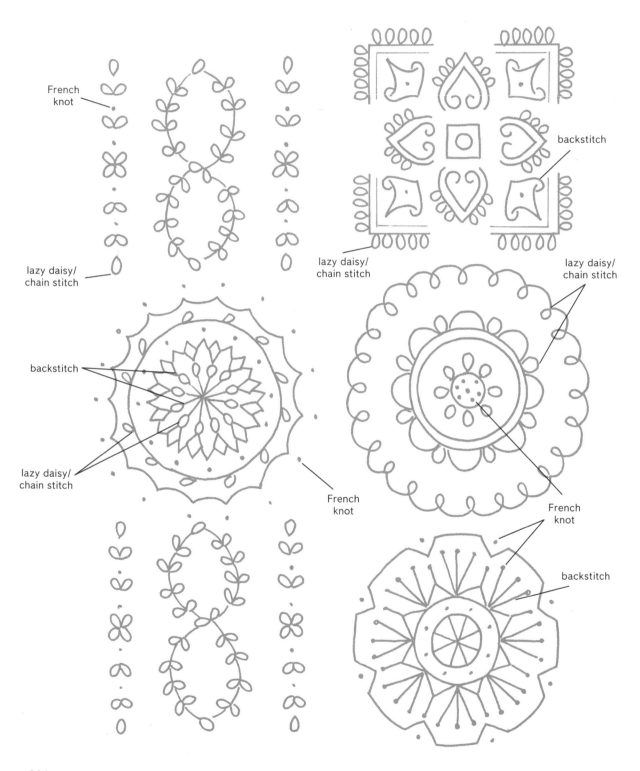

French knot

lazy daisy/ chain stitch

backstitch

lazy daisy/ chain stitch

lazy daisy/ chain stitch

backstitch

lazy daisy/ chain stitch

French knot

French knot

backstitch

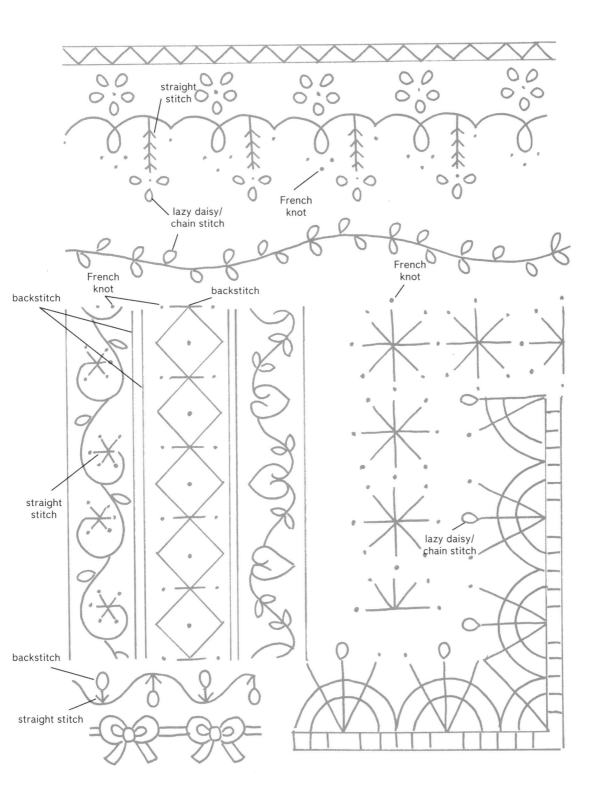

straight stitch

lazy daisy/ chain stitch

French knot

French knot

backstitch

French knot

backstitch

backstitch

straight stitch

French knot

lazy daisy/ chain stitch

backstitch

straight stitch

see project on page 205

^{12.} fairies

see project on page 206

^{13.} shells and starfish

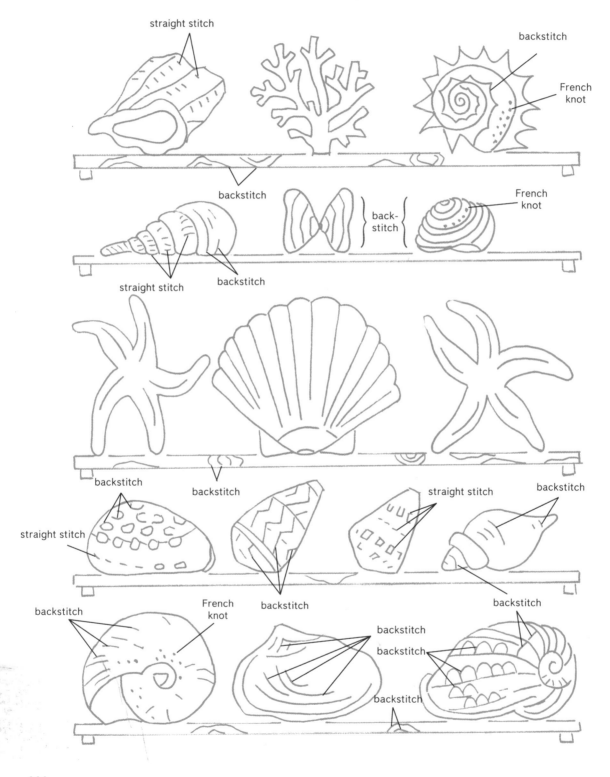

straight stitch

backstitch

French knot

backstitch

straight stitch

backstitch

back-stitch

French knot

backstitch

backstitch

straight stitch

straight stitch

backstitch

backstitch

backstitch

backstitch

French knot

backstitch

backstitch

backstitch

backstitch

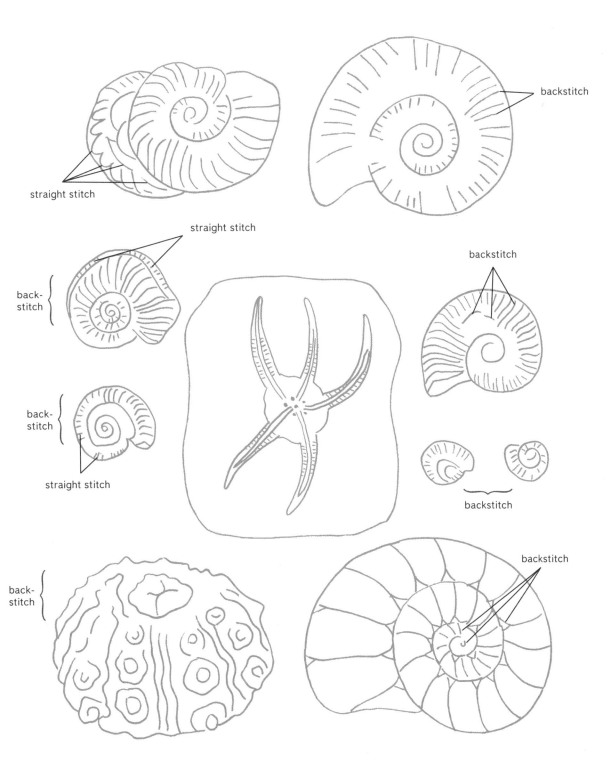

straight stitch

backstitch

straight stitch

back-
stitch

backstitch

back-
stitch

straight stitch

backstitch

back-
stitch

backstitch

see project on page 207

14 & 17. lacy borders

see projects on pages 208 and 211

15. holiday cheer

see project on page 209

16. feathers

see project on page 210

acknowledgments

Thanks to Christine and Natalie for their magic fingers and their fairy touch. . . . and to Christine, Muriel, Hervé and Ethan, Joelle and Pierre, and Valérie and Olivier for opening up their homes to us.

resources

craft supplies

A.C. Moore

www.acmoore.com

1-888-ACMOORE

Hobby Lobby

www.hobbylobby.com

For mail order or online purchasing:

www.craftsetc.com

1-800-888-0321

Jo-Ann

www.joann.com

1-888-739-4120

Michaels

www.michaels.com

1-800-MICHAELS (1-800-642-4235)

embroidery floss

Anchor

www.coatsandclark.com

800-648-1479

To purchase online:

www.theyarncollection.com

.1-877-292-0062

CustomerService-CC@herrschners.com

The Caron Collection

www.caron-net.com

203-381-9999

mail@caron-net.com

Crescent Colors

www.crescentcolors.com

1-888-9-THREAD

DMC

www.dmc-usa.com

973-589-0606

dmcusa@dmcus.com

The Gentle Art

www.thegentleart.com

614-855-8346

Gloriana Hand Dyed Threads

www.glorianathreads.com

425-558-9200

Kreinik

www.kreinik.com

1-800-537-2166

info@kreinik.com

Rainbow Gallery

www.rainbowgallery.com

email@rainbowgallery.com

Weeks Dye Works

www.weeksdyeworks.com

877-OVERDYE

contact@weeksdyeworks.com

YLI

www.ylicorp.com

803-985-3100

ylicorp@ylicorp.com

aida cloth

DMC

www.dmc-usa.com

973-589-0606

dmcusa@dmcus.com

Charles Craft

charlescraft.com

910-844-3521 ext. 351

sbuffkin@charlescraft.com

mzadel@charlescraft.com

Zweigart

www.zweigart.com

732-562-8888

info@zweigart.com

fabric transfer paper

Avery

www.avery.com

1-800-GO-AVERY (800-462-8379)

Epson

www.epson.com

800-873-7799

HP

www.shopping.hp.com

877-204-5259

index

NOTE: Page numbers in GREEN refer to motifs.